ELLA THREADWELL

Animal Pals Crochet

For Beginners

Includes Detailed Video Tutorials

20 Fun and Easy Step-by-Step Patterns for Making Adorable Animals

First Edition

ISBN: 9798333584397

For permissions, contact:
Email: ellathreadwell@gmail.com

Contents

Amigurumi List

Introduction

Have a nice day!

I'm **Ella Threadwell**, a lover of all things yarn and creativity. My journey into the world of crochet began one rainy afternoon when I stumbled upon an old ball of yarn tucked away in a dusty corner of my closet. With nothing else to do, I decided to give crocheting a try. Little did I know, that simple act would open up a world full of color, joy, and endless possibilities.

Crocheting quickly became my favorite pastime. I started with basic projects like scarves and hats, but soon, I found myself wanting to take on more complex challenges. That's when the idea of creating cute animals from yarn struck me – and it was pure magic when my handmade bunnies, bears, and cats brought smiles to my friends and family.

This book, **"Animal Pals Crochet Book for Beginners"** is a result of my passion and continuous creativity. I want to share with you some of my most beloved patterns, each designed to be easy to follow and complete, even if you're just starting out. From a playful penguin to a mischievous lion, each page will guide you through a delightful and fun adventure. The best part about crocheting is that you don't just create beautiful items; you also find relaxation and joy in the process. Let this book be your companion on your creative journey, helping you discover and develop your crocheting skills.

Together, we'll turn simple yarn into charming animal friends full of personality and charm. I'm excited to share this journey with you and can't wait to see the wonderful creations you'll bring to life!

happy crocheting !

Chapter 1

Foundation

Introduction to Crochet and Animal Pals

Crocheting cute animal friends is not just a fun hobby; it's a great way to relax, heal, and boost your creativity. In this chapter, you'll take your first steps into the world of crochet, learning everything you need to know to make adorable amigurumi.

We'll start by exploring the different types of yarn and crochet hooks you'll need for various projects, and you'll see how these materials can influence the final look of your creations. Understanding the different kinds of yarn and their fiber compositions, as well as choosing the right hooks, will help you pick the best supplies for your crocheted animals.

So, get ready to dive in! Gather your tools and yarn, and prepare for a whimsical adventure in crocheting your very own animal friends. This is where your creative journey begins!

Materials and tools

Yarn and Crochet Hook Guide

Each skein of yarn typically comes with a label detailing the fiber composition, usage instructions, and care guidelines. It also suggests appropriate hook sizes.

Small Hooks (< 1.5 mm)

Ideal for delicate threads like lace, cotton, or Thai yarn. Perfect for fine, detailed work such as amigurumi keychains, intricate patterns, or elegant dresses with a soft drape.

Medium Hooks (1.75 mm to 5 mm)

Versatile for a variety of yarns including milk cotton, wool blends, acrylics, and novelty yarns. Suitable for clothing items like pants, tops, dresses, and hats.

Large Hooks (5.5 mm and above)

Best for bulky yarns. Use these for thick, cozy items like blankets, heavy scarves, or coats. They create warm and substantial pieces.

This guide ensures that you choose the right hook for your yarn to achieve the best results in your projects. When crocheting amigurumi, it is important to crochet tightly to prevent the stuffing from showing. Therefore, you should choose a crochet hook that is smaller than the recommended size on the yarn label.

In this collection of 20 Amigurumi Animals, we use milk cotton yarn and crochet hook 4.0mm.

Yarn Sewing Needle

The yarn sewing needle helps connect parts of knitted or crocheted products together and neatly hide any excess yarn ends inside the product.

Positioning Pins

Positioning pins help to hold the parts of your knitted or crocheted product in place while you sew or join them together, ensuring accurate and secure assembly. Additionally, you can use positioning pins to keep parts aligned and prevent them from shifting while you join them together.

Scissors

When crocheting yarn, you should use small, sharp scissors with pointed tips. Scissors specifically designed for crocheting are often referred to as thread snips or embroidery scissors. They help you cut the yarn precisely and neatly, especially when trimming excess yarn or cutting small details. The pointed tips make it easy to cut close to the stitches without damaging the product.

Stuffing

Cotton stuffing is widely used for filling crocheted stuffed animals made with the amigurumi technique. The stuffing helps the products maintain a plump, cute shape and provides a soft feel when held.

To stuff, simply use your hands or a tool to insert the cotton stuffing into the project until you reach the desired firmness. When stuffing, make sure the cotton is evenly distributed to avoid lumps or unevenness.

There are various types of stuffing available to suit your needs and budget.

Glue

Specialized yarn glue is a type of adhesive specifically designed to bond yarn fibers or yarn products together. This glue typically does not harden the yarn after drying and keeps the joints flexible, maintaining the softness of the product. These glues often take a long time to dry, so you can use pins to hold the parts in place while the glue sets.

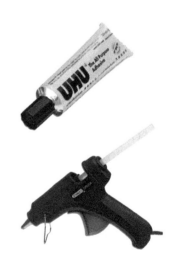

You can also use hot melt glue such as hot glue sticks, if you need immediate adhesion. However, it is advisable to mark the exact positions before attaching the parts because once hot glue sticks, it is difficult to remove.

Abbreviations

MR	Magic Ring
CH	Chain
SC	Single Crochet
INC	Increase
DEC	Decrease
SLST	Slip Stitch
ST	Stitch
FLO	Front Loop Only
BLO	Back Loop Only
SK	Skip
W	3 Single Crochet Together
HDC	Half Double Crochet
TV	Increase (2 Half Double Crochet)
DC	Double Crochet
FV	Increase (2 Double Crochet)
E	Double Treble Crochet

Tips and tricks

For beginners, start with yarn that's easy to work with and a crochet hook that's the right size. Cotton or acrylic yarns are usually great choices to start with.

Keep your hands relaxed while crocheting to avoid straining your muscles. This will help you crochet more evenly and prevent hand pain.

To make sure your project doesn't end up crooked or misshapen, count your stitches often. This is especially crucial when you're just starting out.

Use stitch markers to keep track of your work. Mark the first and last stitch of each row so you don't lose your place. You can use paper clips or special stitch markers for this.

Make sure you're comfortable with basic stitches like chain stitch, single crochet, and double crochet before moving on to more advanced techniques.

If you run into trouble with a pattern, please scan QR code included each chapter for detailed instructions. There are plenty of videos and images that can help you understand the techniques better.

Don't hesitate to experiment with different types of yarn and stitches. This will help you discover your own style and favorite techniques.

Try to keep your stitches even as you work. This will make your finished project look more professional and neat.

Chapter 2

Mastering Basic Crochet Stitches for Animal Pal Projects

(Scan the QR code for detailed instructions)

Mastering Basic Crochet Stitches for Animal Pal Projects

Essential crochet stitch for beginner

In this book, I use Milk Cotton yarn to crochet the 20 amigurumi projects, but I will use fabric yarn to demonstrate the basic stitches to help you see the stitches more clearly. In the next chapter, I'll show you the crochet stitches we'll use to make 20 amigurumi dolls. I'll also introduce some other stitches in future projects. I will include a QR code that links to a video tutorial demonstrating the specific steps for each crochet stitch.

1. Magic Ring

The magic circle ring is a fundamental technique in crochet, allowing you to start projects like circles or tubes neatly and tightly compared to starting with a chain. This technique is often used in projects such as crocheting hats, Amigurumi toys, or any patterns that require starting with a small round.

How to crochet Magic Ring

Step 1: Insert the hook
- Loop the yarn around your fingers as shown in the picture.
- Insert the crochet hook under the yarn looped around your fingers.
- Pull this strand through the loop around your fingers.
- Twist the hook and lift the yarn to tighten it and form a loop on the hook.

To finish the magic circle, usually, a chain is used to close the circle and secure the stitches.

Step 2: Crochet into the Magic Circle
Crochet the required number of single crochet stitches or other types of stitches into the loop depending on your pattern. Typically, you will need 6 to 12 stitches into the loop. (For example, Mr6sc, where "Mr" stands for Magic Ring and "6sc" means six single crochet stitches).

Step 3: Tighten the Yarn to Close the Circle
Gently pull the yarn tail to tighten and close the magic circle, ensuring the stitches are snug and secure.

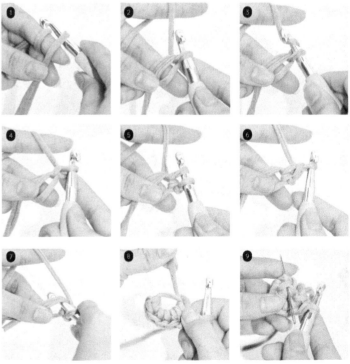

2. Chain – Ch

The chain stitch, often abbreviated as "ch," is a fundamental crochet stitch used to create a base for various projects. It's versatile and frequently used in items like bags, scarves, and more. Depending on the project, the number of chain stitches required will vary.

How to Crochet a Chain Stitch

Step 1: Create a Loop
- Start by making a loop around your finger with the yarn, leaving a short tail hanging down.
- This loop will serve as the starting point for your chain stitches.

Step 2: Insert the Hook and Pull Through
- Insert the crochet hook into the loop.
- Use the hook to grab the working yarn (the longer end connected to the yarn ball) and pull it through the loop.
- This action creates the first chain stitch.

Step 3: Repeat for Additional Chains

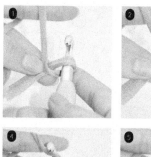 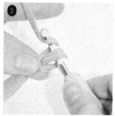 
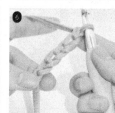

3. Single Crochet – Sc

The single crochet stitch, abbreviated as "sc," is one of the most basic and commonly used stitches in crochet. It creates a dense and sturdy fabric, making it ideal for a wide range of projects, including blankets, garments, and Amigurumi toys.
There are two types: V-stitch single crochet and X-stitch single crochet (X-stitch is often preferred for its higher aesthetic appeal).

How to Crochet a Single Crochet stitch

For single crochet, insert the hook into the loop, pull the working yarn through the loop, then pull the yarn through both loops on the hook.

Single Crochet from a Chain:
Skip the first chain closest to the hook (this is the turning chain, and it doesn't count as a stitch) and insert the hook into the second chain from the hook. Yarn over and pull through the chain. You will now have two loops on the hook.
Yarn over again and pull through both loops on the hook.

 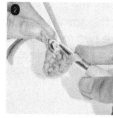

Single Crochet from a Magic Ring:
After creating the magic ring, pull the yarn through the ring to make a loop on the hook. Yarn over again and pull through both loops on the hook. This is your first single crochet stitch. Continue to single crochet into the ring until you have the required number of stitches, then tighten the ring.

  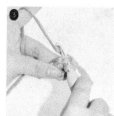

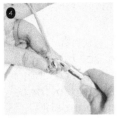

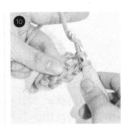
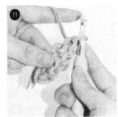

4. 3 Single Crochet Together – W/SC3TOG

The "3 Single Crochet Together" stitch is used to decrease three stitches into one stitch. This creates a tighter, more gathered effect in your crochet work, which is particularly useful for shaping or creating a more defined look in your patterns.

How to crochet 3 Single Crochet Together stitch

Insert your hook into the specified stitch and yarn over. Pull the yarn through the stitch to create two loops on your hook. Yarn over again and pull through both loops to complete the first single crochet. Insert your hook back into the same stitch, yarn over, and pull through to create two loops again. Yarn over and pull through both loops to complete the second single crochet. Repeat this process one more time for the third single crochet.

How to Weave in Yarn Ends After 3 Single Crochet Together Stitch

After finishing 3 single crochet stitches into one stitch, cut the yarn leaving a tail of about 10-15 cm (4-6 inches) and thread it onto a yarn needle. Starting from the back of the stitch cluster, weave the yarn needle through the surrounding stitches or in a zigzag pattern to secure the end. Continue weaving the yarn through a few more stitches to ensure it stays in place. Check the tension to make sure the yarn is neither too tight nor too loose, then trim any excess yarn

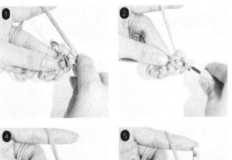

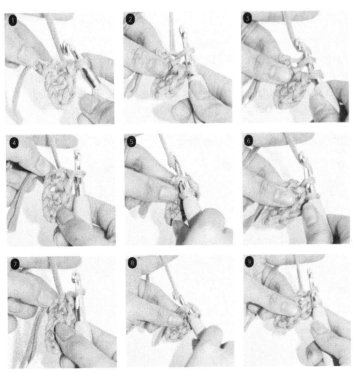

5. Increase – Inc/SC2TOG

In crochet, an increase stitch is used to add extra stitches to a row or round, helping to shape the project by creating more volume or expanding certain areas. This technique is essential for making items like amigurumi, hats, and other complex patterns.

How to crochet Increase stitch

First, after crocheting a single crochet stitch into a stitch from the previous row, you continue by crocheting another single crochet stitch into the same stitch. This creates two single crochet stitches in the same stitch from the previous row, effectively increasing the stitch count in your row. This technique is commonly used to create curved shapes and expand crochet patterns.

Do the same with the 3 and 4 crochet stitches together.

6. Decrease – Dec

"Decrease stitch" abbreviated as "dec" refers to a crochet technique used to reduce the number of stitches in a row. It is commonly employed to shape or smoothly finish parts of a crochet project, ensuring even and tidy results.

How to Crochet a Decrease stitch

Insert the hook into the back loop of the first stitch, then into the back loop of the next stitch, yarn over, and crochet as a regular single crochet stitch. This technique is also known as invisible decrease, helping to create a neater and less visible stitch in crochet work.

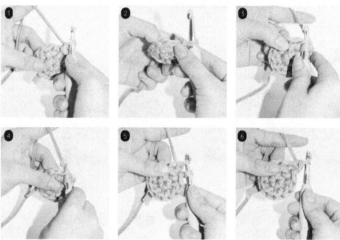

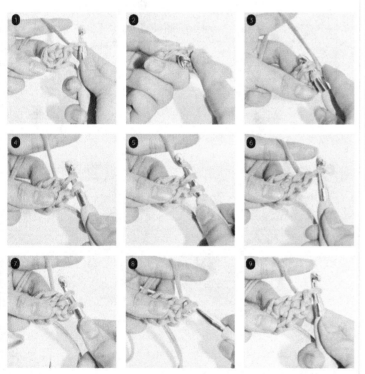

7. Front Loop Only – FLO

"Front Loop Only" (FLO) refers to a crochet technique where you work into only the front loop of a stitch, rather than both loops (front and back) as you normally would. This technique is commonly used to create texture or special effects in crochet patterns.

How to crochet Front Loop Only stitch

Observe each stitch in the previous row. You will see two loops at the top of the stitch: the front loop and the back loop. Insert your hook into only the front loop of the stitch, leaving the back loop unworked. Yarn over and pull through the front loop to complete the stitch, whether it's a single crochet or any other stitch required by your pattern.

8. Back Loop Only – BLO

"Back Loop Only" (BLO) is a crochet technique where you work into only the back loop of the stitch from the previous row, leaving the front loop unworked. This method creates raised lines or adds texture to your crochet project.

How to crochet Back Loop Only stitch

Look at each stitch in the previous row. You'll see two loops at the top of the stitch: the front loop and the back loop. The back loop is the one further from you when viewed from above. Insert your hook into only the back loop of the stitch, skipping the front loop. Yarn over and pull through the back loop to complete the stitch, such as a single crochet or any other stitch required by your pattern.

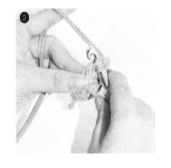
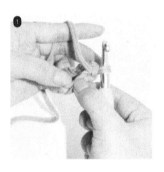
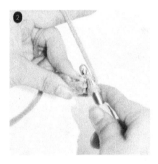

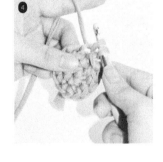

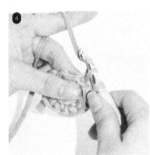

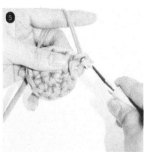
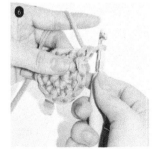
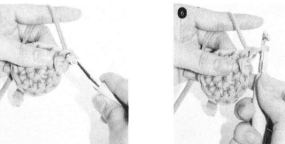
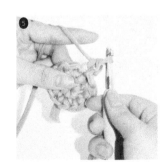

9. Skip – Sk

"Skip" means to pass over one or more stitches in the current or previous row. This basic technique is often used in many crochet patterns to create spaces, change shapes, or adjust the size of the project. By skipping stitches, you can change the width or thickness of the crochet piece.

How to do Skip stitch

Instead of inserting the hook into the next stitch as usual, you will jump over the specified number of stitches. For example, if the pattern says "skip 1 stitch," you will skip the next stitch and insert your hook into the 2nd stitch. If the pattern says "skip 2 stitches," you will skip the next two stitches and insert your hook into the third stitch.

10. Slip stitch – sl st

Slip stitch crochet is one of the basic crochet stitches, characterized by its small size and the fact that it doesn't add height to your work. Slip stitches are commonly used to join other stitches together, or to create borders, curves, or closed shapes.

How to crochet Slip Stitch

To make a slip stitch, insert the hook into the stitch you want to work into (this could be the next stitch in the row or round you are working on). Yarn over the hook, pull the yarn through the stitch and then through the loop already on your hook. Now you have completed a slip stitch.

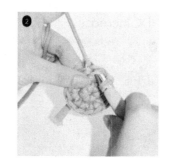
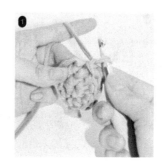
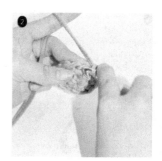

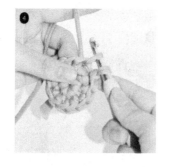
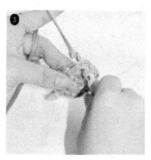
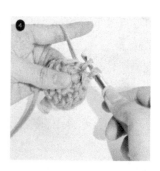

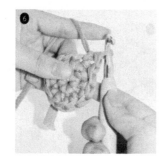
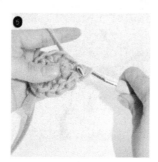
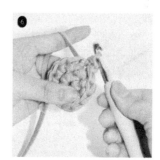

11. Half Double Crochet – hdc

The "Half Double Crochet" (HDC) stitch is a fundamental crochet stitch that falls between a single crochet (SC) and a double crochet (DC) in terms of height and tightness. HDC stitches are versatile and commonly used in various crochet projects to create a balanced texture and density.

How to crochet HDC stitch

Wrap the yarn over your crochet hook from back to front. Insert your hook into the next stitch or designated space. Wrap the yarn over your hook from back to front. Pull this yarn over through the stitch. You should now have three loops on your crochet hook. Wrap the yarn over your hook once more and draw it through all three loops on the hook in one motion.

12. Increase (2 Half Double Crochet) – TV

Increase (2 Half Double Crochet) in crochet is used to increase the number of Half Double Crochet (HDC) stitches in each row. By working two HDC stitches into the same stitch from the previous row, you create an increase point, helping your crochet pattern expand and achieve the desired shape.

How to crochet TV stitch

To do this, after completing one HDC into the stitch from the previous row, you continue by making another HDC into the same stitch. This means you insert your hook into the next stitch on the row, yarn over and pull up a loop (3 loops on hook), yarn over again, insert your hook into the same stitch, yarn over and pull up a loop (5 loops on hook). Yarn over and pull through all loops on the hook to complete the HDC increase.

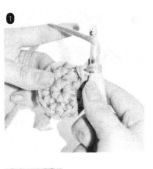
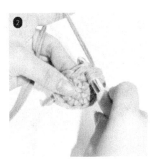
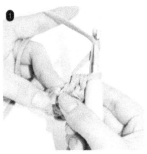

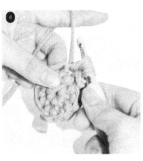
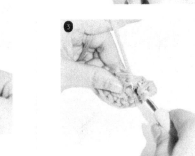
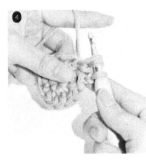

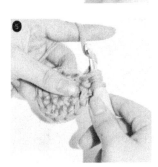
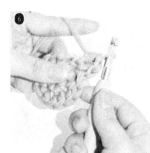

13. Double Crochet – dc/DC2TOG

The Double Crochet stitch, abbreviated as DC, is a versatile and popular stitch in crochet. The double crochet stitch is taller than the single crochet, resulting in a looser, more open fabric, suitable for projects like blankets, garments, and shawls where a lighter, airier texture is desired.

How to crochet DC stitch

This stitch is created by wrapping the yarn around the hook, inserting it into the specified stitch, yarn over again, and drawing through the stitch. You then yarn over and draw through the first two loops on the hook, yarn over again, and draw through the remaining two loops.
Continue this process for each stitch across the row.
Do the same with the 3 and 4 crochet stitches together.

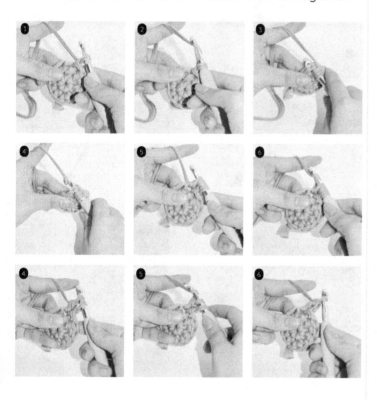

14. Increase (2 Double Crochet) – FV

The Increase (2 Double Crochet) technique in crochet is used to expand the number of Double Crochet (DC) stitches in each row. By working two DC stitches into the same stitch from the previous row, you can quickly and effectively enlarge your crochet pattern.

How to crochet FV stitch

After completing one DC stitch into the previous row's stitch, continue by making another DC stitch into the same stitch. This method creates increase points, shaping the desired form and structure for your crochet project. This technique ensures that your crochet pattern achieves the durability and solidity necessary to complete beautiful and professional designs.
Do the same with the 3 and 4 crochet stitches together.

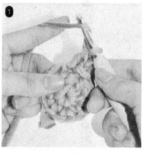
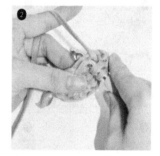
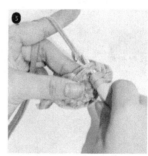
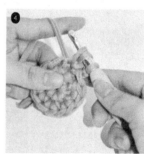
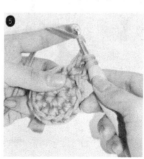
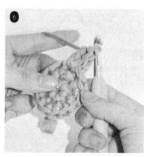

15. Double Treble Crochet – e

The Double Treble Crochet is one of the tallest and most open stitches in crochet. It's significantly taller than basic stitches. This stitch is often used to create lacy patterns or to add height to crochet projects. The Double Treble Crochet creates a loose and airy texture. Therefore, it's suitable for making lace patterns, shawls, or details that need a soft and light finish.

How to crochet Double Treble Crochet stitch

To crochet a Double Treble Crochet stitch, start by chaining four stitches. Then, yarn over the hook three times and insert the hook into the next stitch. Yarn over again and pull through the first set of two loops on the hook, repeating until two loops remain. Finally, yarn over and pull through the last two loops to complete the DTR stitch.

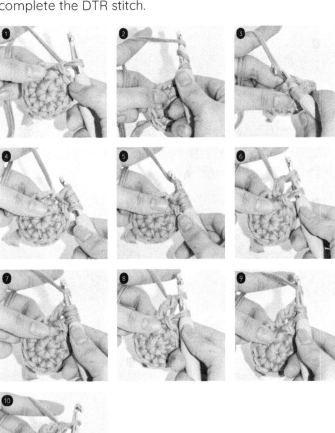

16. Finishing round

Ensure even stitch alignment: After finishing one round of stitches, at the last stitch, insert a slip stitch into the first stitch to close the circle.

For the second round, start by chaining one stitch to begin the new round. Insert the hook into the first stitch, right at the same position where you previously inserted the slip stitch. This will ensure that the alignment of the stitches is even, and the rounds will not be off-center

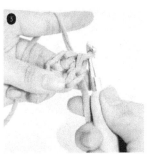
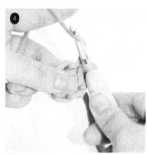
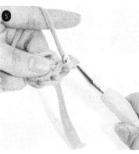

Chapter 3

Creating Your Animals

(Scan the QR code for detailed instructions)

Water the Elephant

(Difficult level 🧶 🧶 🧶 🧶)

Little elephant Water lives in a zoo, and he always attracts attention with his special hobby of bathing every morning. Whenever the zookeepers turn on the water hose, Water eagerly dances under the cool stream. It's said that whenever Water finishes bathing, everyone feels like they've watched a lively performance, with Water as the star of the show!

Materials

- Yarns (milk cotton): grey, white, red, cyan blue
- Stuffing
- Safety eyes: 6mm
- Crochet hook 4.

Size

Approximately 2.7 inches wide by 4.7 inches tall

Skills

Magic ring (13), Single Crochet (15), Increase (17), Decrease (17), Slip Stitch (19), Chain (15), Single Crochet 4 Together (16).

Head

Round 1: Mr6sc
Round 2: 6sc (12)
Round 3: (sc, inc) repeat 6 times (18)
Round 4: (2sc, inc) repeat 6 times (24)
Round 5: (3sc, inc) repeat 6 times (30)
Round 6: (4sc, inc) repeat 6 times (36)
Round 7: 36sc
Round 8: (5sc, inc) repeat 6 times (42)
Round 9-13: 42sc (42)
Round 14: (5sc, dec) repeat 6 times (36)
Round 15: (4sc, dec) repeat 6 times (30)
Round 16: (3sc, dec) repeat 6 times (24)
Round 17: (2sc, dec) repeat 6 times (18)

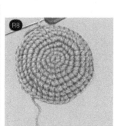

--- NOTE ---------------

Stuff until full

Body

Round 1: Mr6sc
Round 2: 6sc (12)
Round 3: (sc, inc) repeat 6 times (18)
Round 4: (2sc, inc) repeat 6 times (24)
Round 5: (3sc, inc) repeat 6 times (30)
Round 6: (4sc, inc) repeat 6 times (36)
Round 7-9: 36sc (36)
Round 10: (4sc, dec) repeat 6 times (30)
Round 11: 30sc (30)
Round 12: (3sc, dec) repeat 6 times (24)
Round 13: (2sc, dec) repeat 6 times (18)

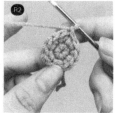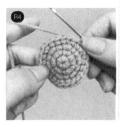

Connect the body and head: Sew on the inside

Trunk

Round 1: Mr4sc
Round 2: sc, 2inc, sc (6)
Round 3-4: dec, sc, inc, 2sc (6)
Round 5: 2sc, 2inc, 2sc (8)
Round 6: dec, 2sc, inc, 3sc (8)

  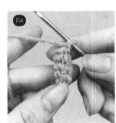

Ears

Start with white yarn

Round 1: Mr4sc
Round 2: 4inc (8)

Change to grey yarn

Round 3: 8inc (16)
Round 4: 2ch, slst

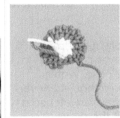 

Arms and Legs

Round 1: Mr6sc
Round 2: (sc, inc) repeat 3 times (9)
Round 3-6: 9sc
Round 7: 9sc, slst

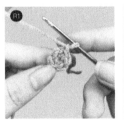 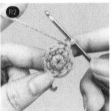 

Bib

Sart with red yarn
Round 1: 3ch, sc, SC4TOG, sc

Change to white yarn
Round 2: inc, sc, 2inc, sc, inc (10)

Change to green yarn
Round 3: 3sc, (sc, inc) repeat 2 times, 3sc (12)

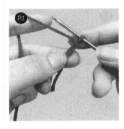 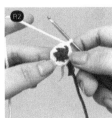 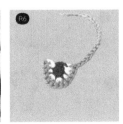

Finish

- Attach the safety eyes (between R9&10) and the trunk to the head.
- Attach the arms and legs to the body.
- Wear the Bib.

SCAN ME

Pippin The Dinosaur

Difficult level 🧶🧶🧶🧶

Pippin made mistakes that affected his friends because of his greediness and selfishness. However, in the end, Pippin realized his mistakes and worked to correct them. He started living more harmoniously and learned to share with others. Pippin also realized that he needs to lose weight right away!

Materials

- Yarns (milk cotton): pink, grey
- Stuffing
- Safety eyes: 8mm
- Crochet hook 4.

Size

Aapproximately 2.8 inches wide by 5.2 inches tall

Skills

Magic ring (14), Single Crochet (15), Increase (17), Decrease (17)

Head

Round 1: Mr8sc
Round 2: 8inc (16)
Round 3: (sc, inc) repeat 8 times (24)
Round 4: (2sc, inc) repeat 8 times (32)
Round 5: (3sc, inc) repeat 8 times (40)
Round 6: (4sc, inc) repeat 8 times (48)
Round 7-10: 48sc
Round 11: (7sc, inc) repeat 6 times (54)
Round 12-17: 54sc
Round 18: (7sc, dec) repeat 6 times (48)
Round 19: (4sc, dec) repeat 8 times (40)
Round 20: (3sc, dec) repeat 8 times (32)
Round 21: (2sc, dec) repeat 8 times (24)
Round 22: (sc, dec) repeat 8 times (16)

NOTE

Stuff until full

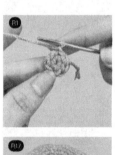  

Round 23: 8dec (8)
Round 24: 4dec (4)

Body

Round 1: Mr8sc
Round 2: 8inc (16)
Round 3: (sc, inc) repeat 8 times (24)
Round 4: (2sc, inc) repeat 8 times (32)
Round s: (3sc, inc) repeat 8 times (40)
Round 6: (4sc, inc) repeat 8 times (48)
Round 7: (5sc, inc) repeat 8 times (56)
Round 8-12: 56sc
Round 13: (5sc, dec) repeat 8 times (48)
Round 14-16: 48sc
Round 17: (6sc, dec) repeat 6 times (42)
Round 18: (5sc, dec) repeat 6 times (36)

- NOTE

Stuff until full

Round 8: (6sc, inc) repeat 3 times (24)
Round 9: (7sc, inc) repeat 3 times (27)
Round 10: (8sc, inc) repeat 3 times (30)

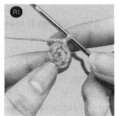  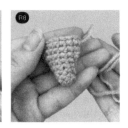

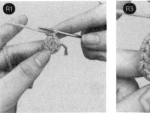  

Arms

Round 1: Mr6sc
Round 2: (sc, inc) repeat 3 times (9)
Round 3-4: 9sc

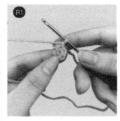 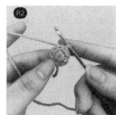 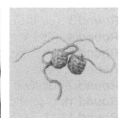

Legs

Round 1: Mr6sc
Round 2: 6inc (12)
Round 3-4: 12sc

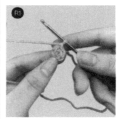  

Tail

Round 1: Mr6sc
Round 2: (2sc, inc) repeat 2 times (8)
Round 3: (3sc, inc) repeat 2 times (10)
Round 4: (4sc, inc) repeat 2 times (12)
Round 5: (3sc, inc) repeat 3 times (15)
Round 6: (4sc, inc) repeat 3 times (18)
Round 7: (5sc, inc) repeat 3 times (21)

Back Spikes

Round 1: Mr7sc
Round 2: 7inc (14)
Round 3-4: 14sc

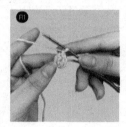 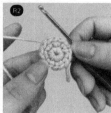 

Finish

- Connect the body and head: Sew the head so that the dinosaur's head is lifted up.
- Attach the safety eyes to the head.
- Attach the Back Spikes from the top of the head to the bottom

SCAN ME

Snowball The Hippo

(Difficult level 🧶🧶🧶🧶🧶)

Snowball, the playful white hippo, loved rolling down grassy hills. One sunny day, he rolled right into a puddle, surprising a group of monkeys. They laughed and helped Snowball out and taught him how to swing from vines.

Materials

- Yarns (milk cotton): white
- Thread: Black
- Stuffing
- Safety eyes: 8mm
- Crochet hook 4.

Size

Approximately 3.5 inches wide by 6.3 inches tall

Skills

Magic ring (14), Single Crochet (15), Increase (17), Decrease (17), 3 Single Crochet Together (16), Chain (15), Double Crochet 3 Together (21), Back Loop Only (18), Slip Stitch (19)

Body

Round 1: Mr6sc
Round 2: 6inc
Round 3: (sc, inc) repeat 6 times
Round 4: (sc, inc, sc) repeat 6 times
Round 5: (3sc, inc) repeat 6 times
Round 6: (2sc, inc, 2sc) repeat 6 times
Round 7: (5sc, inc) repeat 6 times
Round 8: (3sc, inc, 3sc) repeat 6 times
Round 9-12: 48sc
Round 13: (7sc, dec) repeat 3 times, 21sc
Round 14: 45sc
Round 15: (6sc, dec) repeat 3 times, 21sc
Round 16-17: 42sc
Round 18: (5sc, dec) repeat 6 times
Round 19: 36sc
Round 20: (2sc, dec, 2sc) repeat 6 times
Round 21: 30sc
Round 22: (3sc, dec) repeat 6 times
Round 23: 24sc

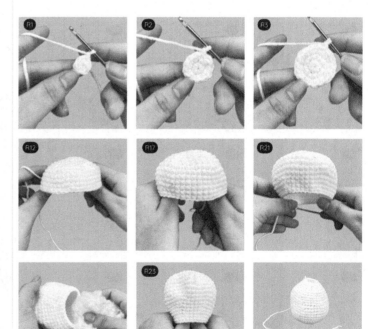

 NOTE

Stuff until full

Round 24: (sc, dec, sc) repeat 6 times
Round 25: 18sc

Head

Round 1: 7ch, the 2nd st from the hook:
5sc, W, 4sc, inc
Round 2: (inc, 4sc, 2inc) repeat 2 times
Round 3: (inc, 5sc, inc, sc, inc, sc) repeat 2 times
Round 4: (sc, inc, 6sc, inc, 2sc, inc, sc) repeat 2 times
Round 5: (sc, inc, 7sc, inc, 3sc, inc, 2sc) repeat 2 times
Round 6-12: 38sc
Round 13: (dec, 7sc, dec, 3sc, dec, 3sc) repeat 2 times
Round 14: 17sc, 4dec, 7sc
Round 15: 16sc, 3dec, 6sc
Round 16: 25sc
Round 17: (2sc, inc, 2sc) repeat 5 times
Round 18-22: 30sc
Round 23: (2sc, dec, 2sc) repeat 5 times

NOTE

Stuff until full

Round 24: (3sc, dec) repeat 5 times
Round 25: (sc, dec, sc) repeat 5 times
Round 26: 7dec, sc

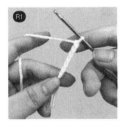
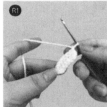
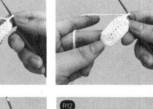

Ears

Round 1: Mr5sc
Round 2: 5inc
Round 3: (sc, inc) repeat 5 times
Round 4: 15sc

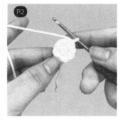

Arms

Round 1: Mr5sc
Round 2: 5inc
Round 3: 10sc
Round 4: 1ch, DC3TOG, 9sc
Round 5: sl st, 9sc
Round 6: (3sc, dec) repeat 2 times
Round 7-15: 8sc

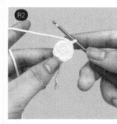
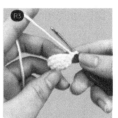
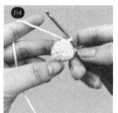

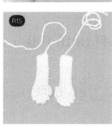

Legs

Round 1: Mr5sc
Round 2: 5inc
Round 3: (sc, inc) repeat 5 times
Round 4: BLO15sc
Round 5: 15sc
Round 6: 5sc, 3dec, 4sc
Round 7: 4sc, 2dec, 4sc
Round 8: 10sc
Round 9: (sc, inc) repeat 5 times
Round 10: 15sc

NOTE
Stuff until full

 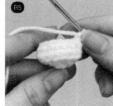 

Tail

26ch, the 2nd st from the hook: 25sl

Finish

- Connect the body and head: Sew on the inside
- Attach the safety eyes to the head.
- Sew the arms and legs to the body.
- Sew the eyebrows by Black thread.

SCAN ME

Baobao The Panda

Difficult level

The adorable Baobao, absolutely loves strawberries and usually visits a small strawberry patch behind the bamboo forest. One day, a mouse startled Baobao, causing her to accidentally knock over her entire basket of strawberries. She became very angry and made the mouse pick up all the spilled strawberries back into the basket!

Materials

- Yarns (milk cotton): black, white, red, green
- Thread: Black
- Stuffing
- Safety eyes: 6mm
- Crochet hook 4.

Size
Approximately 2.8 inches wide by 4.3 inches tall

Skills
Magic ring (14), Single Crochet (15), Increase (17), Decrease (170, 3 Single Crochet Together (16), Chain (15), Changing colors

Head

Round 1: 6sc
Round 2: 6inc
Round 3: (sc, inc) repeat 6 times
Round 4: (sc, inc, sc) repeat 6 times
Round 5: (3sc, inc) repeat 6 times
Round 6: (2sc, inc, 2sc) repeat 6 times
Round 7-9: 36sc
Round 10: 10sc, 5inc, 6sc, 5inc, 10sc
Round 11-13: 46sc
Round 14: 10sc, 5dec, 6sc, 5dec, 10sc
Round 15: (2sc, dec, 2sc) repeat 6 times
Round 16: (3sc, dec) repeat 6 times

- NOTE

Stuff until full

Round 17: (2sc, dec, 2sc) repeat 6 times

Legs + Body

Start with black yarn

Round 1: 6sc
Round 2: inc, 4sc, inc
Round 3: 8sc

Make 2 pieces, connect 2 legs by 3ch

Round 4: Change to white yarn, 22sc
Round 5: sc, inc, 3sc, (sc, inc) repeat 4 times, 3sc, (sc, inc) repeat 3 times
Round 6: 30sc
Round 7: 12sc, inc, 14sc, inc, 2sc
Round 8-10: 32sc
Round 11: Change to black yarn, (3sc, dec, 3sc) repeat 4 times
Round 12: 28sc
Round 13: (5sc, dec) repeat 4 times

```
- NOTE
Stuff until full
Connect the body and head:
Sew on the inside
```

Shoulder bag

Round 1: 5ch
Round 2: 3sc, w, 2sc, inc

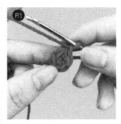 

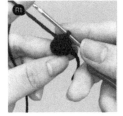 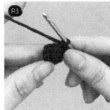 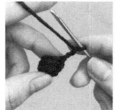

Strawberry leaf

Round 1: Mr4ch
Round 2: Make a loop with the string, repeat this 3 times, and then tighten the loops.

Arms

Round 1: Black, 6sc
Round 2: (sc, inc) repeat 3 times
Round 3: 9sc
Round 4: (sc, dec) repeat 3 times
Round 5-7: 6sc

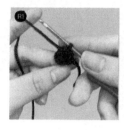  

Ears

Round 1: 6sc
Round 2: 6inc
Round 3: (3sc, inc) repeat 3 times
Round 4: 15sc

Dark circles

Round 1: 5ch
Round 2: 3sc, w, 2sc, inc

Finish

- Attach the dark circles to the head.
- Attach the safety eyes and ears to the head.
- Attach the arms and legs to the body.
- Sew the mouth by Black thread.
- Wear the bag.

SCAN ME

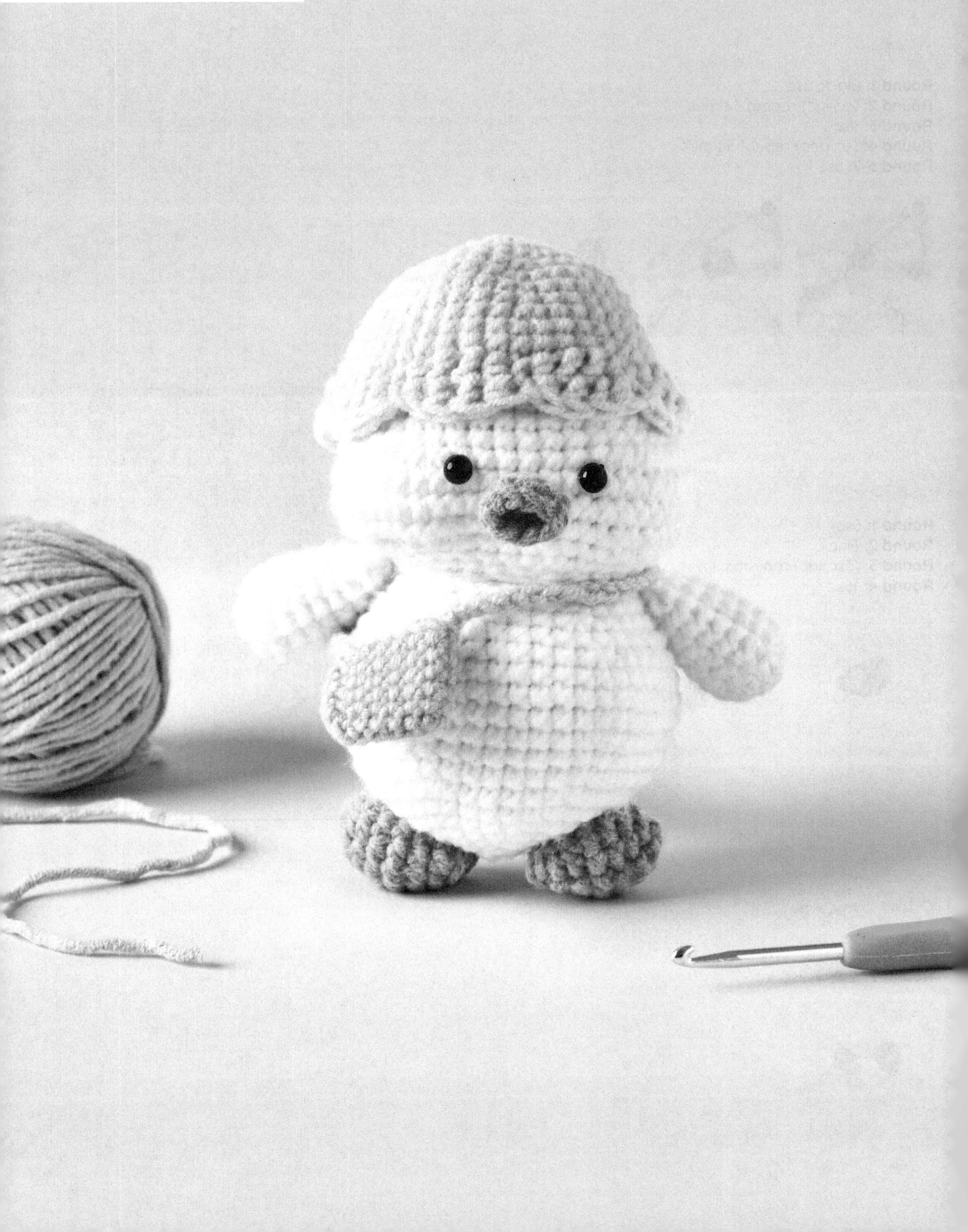

Duckie The Duck

Difficult level

Duckie the duckling is always curious about everything he encounters on his way. Therefore, his mother allowed him to go to school with his friends. Duckie studies very diligently, and he dreams of becoming the best teacher in the world!

Materials

- Yarns (milk cotton): yellow, pink, white, orange
- Stuffing
- Safety eyes: 6mm
- Crochet hook 4.

Size
Approximately 2.8 inches wide by 5.2 inches tall

Skill
Magic ring (14), Single Crochet (15), Increase (17), Decrease (17), Front Loop Only (18), Changing colors

Legs

<u>Make 2 pieces</u>

Round 1: Mr5sc
Round 2: 5inc (10)
Round 3: 10sc
Round 4: (sc, inc) repeat 5 times (15)
Round 5: 15sc
Round 6: (sc, dec) repeat 5 times (10)

- NOTE

Stuff until full

Round 7: 5dec

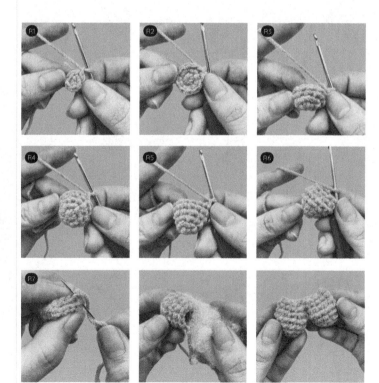

Head

Round 1: Mr6sc
Round 2: 6inc (12)
Round 3: (sc, inc) repeat 6 times (18)
Round 4: (2sc, inc) repeat 6 times (24)
Round 5: (3sc, inc) repeat 6 times (30)
Round 6: (4sc, inc) repeat 6 times (36)
Round 7-8: 36sc
Round 9: (5sc, inc) repeat 6 times (42)
Round 10-12: 42sc
Round 13: 11sc, 6inc, 7sc, 6inc, 12sc (54)
Round 14-16: 54sc
Round 17: 11sc, 6dec, 7sc, 6dec, 12sc (42)
Round 18: (5sc, dec) repeat 6 times (36)
Round 19: (4sc, dec) repeat 6 times (30)

> **NOTE**
> **Cut the yarn and stuff until full**

Mouth

Round 1: Mr8sc
Round 2: 8sc

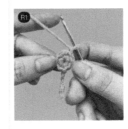
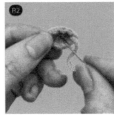

Wings

Make 2 pieces

Round 1: Mr6sc
Round 2: 6inc (12)
Round 3-9: 12sc

> **NOTE**
> **Cut the yarn and stuff until full**
> **Sew it up.**

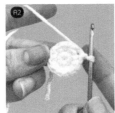
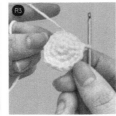

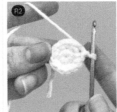

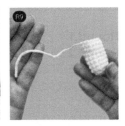

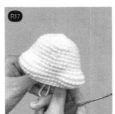
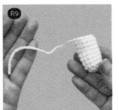

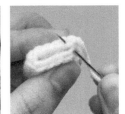

Body

Round 1: Mr6sc
Round 2: 6inc (12)
Round 3: (sc, inc) repeat 6 times (18)
Round 4: (2sc, inc) repeat 6 times (24)
Round 5: (3sc, inc) repeat 6 times (30)
Round 6: (4sc, inc) repeat 6 times (36)
Round 7: (5sc, inc) repeat 6 times (42)
Round 8-9: 42sc
Round 10: (6sc, inc) repeat 6 times (48)
Round 11-13: 48sc
Round 14: (6sc, dec) repeat 6 times (42)
Round 15: 42sc
Round 16: (5sc, dec) repeat 6 times (36)
Round 17: (4sc, inc) repeat 6 times (30)

NOTE
Cut the yarn and stuff until full
Connect the body and head: Sew on the inside

Round 7-8: 36sc
Round 9: (5sc, inc) repeat 6 times (42)
Round 10-11: 42sc
Round 12: FLO sc, (sc, hdc, 2dc, hdc) repeat 8 times, sc
Round 13: sc, (slst, hdc, 2dc, hdc) repeat 8 times, sc

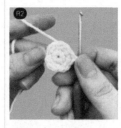

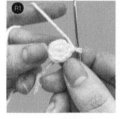
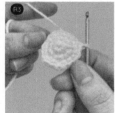
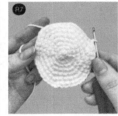

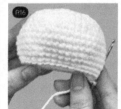

Bag

Round 1: 7ch
Round 2-5: 12sc
Round 6: 50ch

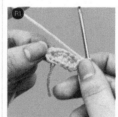
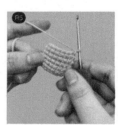

Hat

Round 1: Mr6sc
Round 2: 6inc (12)
Round 3: (sc, inc) repeat 6 times (18)
Round 4: (2sc, inc) repeat 6 times (24)
Round 5: (3sc, inc) repeat 6 times (30)
Round 6: (4sc, inc) repeat 6 times (36)

Finish

- Sew the mouth and eyebrows by Black thread.
- Attach the safety eyes to the head.

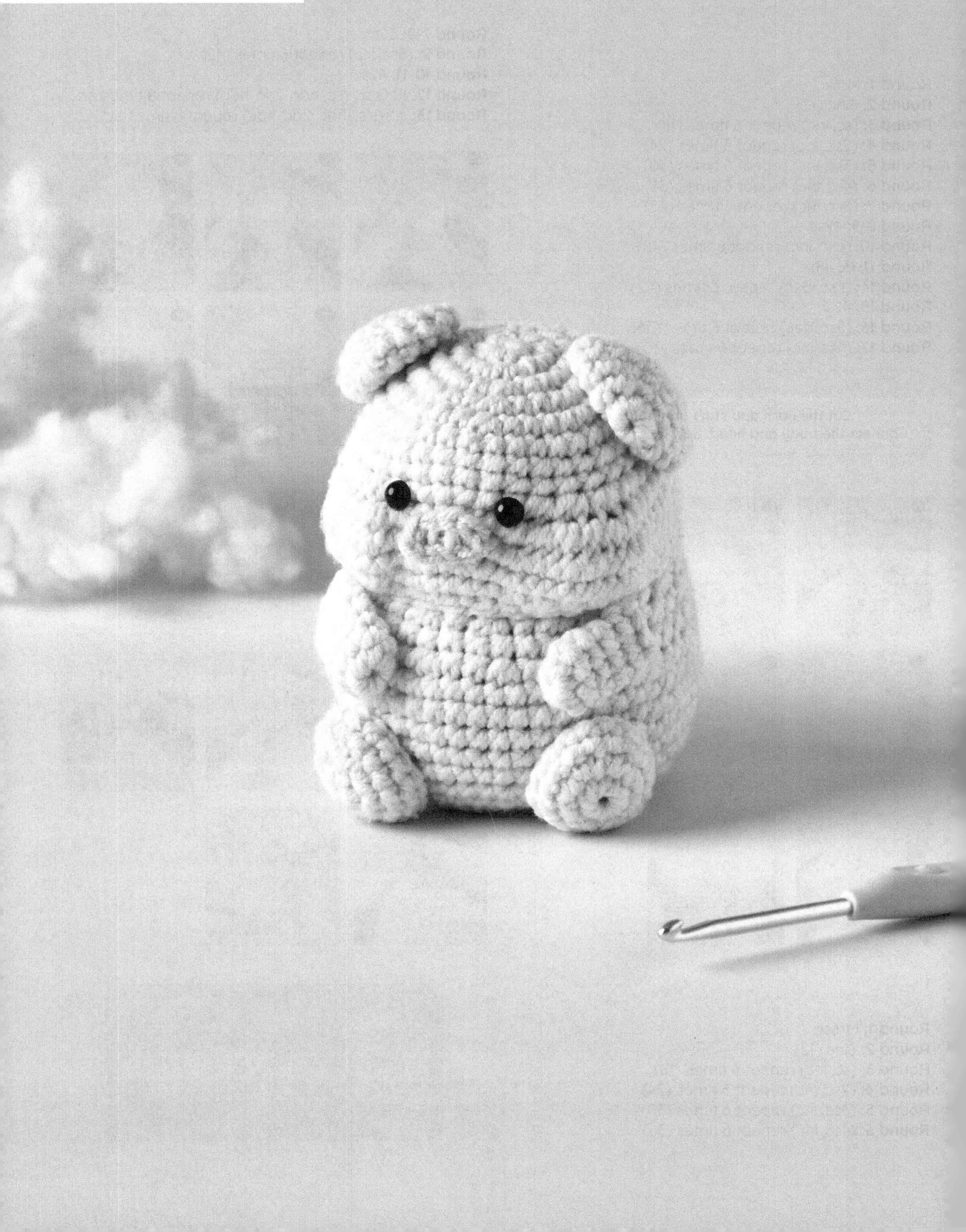

Piggy the pig

Difficult level

At 2 PM, the little piglet headed to the park. Piggy was over the moon with excitement about the swing rides and the carousel. He got so caught up in the fun that he didn't come home until late at night. His dad was furious!

Materials

- Yarns (milk cotton): light pink, dark pink
- Thread: White
- Stuffing
- Safety eyes: 6mm
- Crochet hook 4.

Size
Approximately 3 inches wide by 4 inches tall

Skills
Magic ring (14), Single Crochet (15), Increase (17), Decrease (17), Skip (19), Slip Stitch (19)

Legs

Round 1: Mr8sc
Round 2: 8inc
Round 3-4: 16sc

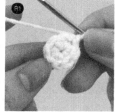  

Nose

5ch, 3sc, w, 2sc, inc.

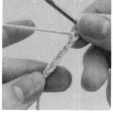  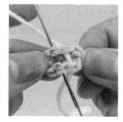

Ears

Round 1: Mr8sc
Round 2: (sc, inc) repeat 4 times
Round 3: (sc, inc, sc) repeat 4 times
Round 4: 16sc

 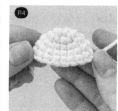 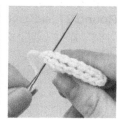

Arms

Round 1: Mr8sc
Round 2-6: 8sc

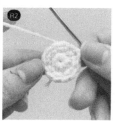  

Head + Body

Round 1: Mr8sc
Round 2: 8inc
Round 3: (sc, inc) repeat 8 times
Round 4: (sc, inc, sc) repeat 8 times
Round 5: (7sc, inc) repeat 4 times
Round 6-8: 36sc
Round 9: 11sc, 4inc, 6sc, 4inc, 11sc
Round 10: 13sc, 6inc, sc, 2dec, sc, 6inc, 13sc
Round 11 - 12: 54sc
Round 13: 13sc, 6dec, 4sc, 6dec, 13sc
Round 14: 12sc, (dec, sc) repeat 3 times, (sc, dec) repeat 3 times, 12sc
Round 15: 10x, dec, sc, dec, 6sc, dec, sc, dec, 10sc
Round 16: 8sc, (sc, inc) repeat 8 times, 8sc
Round 17: 40sc
Round 18: 8sc, (sc, inc, sc) repeat 3 times, 8sc
Round 19-21: 48sc
Round 22: 3sc, 6inc, 32sc, 6inc, sc
Round 23-26: 60sc
Round 27: sk5 and start crocheting on 6th st. 5dec, 2sc, (2sc, dec, 2sc) repeat 5 times, 2sc, 5dec, sc .
Round 28: (3sc, dec) repeat 8 times

NOTE

Stuff until full

Round 29: (sc, dec, sc) repeat 8 times
Round 30: (sc, dec) repeat 8 times
Round 31: 8dec

Sew the bottom closed and cut the yarn

Finish

- Sew the nose to the head.
- Sew the 2 arms and 2 legs onto the body.
- Attach the safety eyes to the head.

SCAN ME

Daisie The Bear

Difficult level

Once upon a time in a quiet forest, there lived a brown bear named Daisie who had a sweet tooth for honey. Every morning, Daisie would venture out with her trusty black scarf to find the juiciest beehives. Her friends often teased her for her love of honey, but Daisie didn't mind - she believed a bit of sweetness made life more enjoyable.

Materials

- Yarns (milk cotton): black, brown
- Thread: Black
- Stuffing
- Safety eyes: 6mm
- Crochet hook 4.

Size
Approximately 2.5 inches wide by 3.5 inches tall

Skills
Magic ring (14), Single Crochet (15), Increase (17), Decrease (17), Back Loop Only (18), Double Crochet (21), Half Double Crochet (20), 3 Single Crochet Together (16)

Ears

Round 1: Mr6sc
Round 2: 6inc
Round 3-4: 12sc

Arms

Round 1: Mr6sc
Round 2: (sc, inc) repeat 3 times
Round 3: (sc, dec) repeat 3 times
Round 4: 6sc

Sew it up

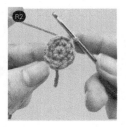 

Legs

Round 1: Mr6sc
Round 2: 6inc
Round 3: 4sc, 2dec, 4sc
Round 4: 10sc
Round 5: 4sc, dec, 4sc
Round 6: 9sc
Round 7: (sc, dec) repeat 3 times

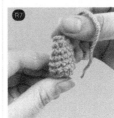

Head and body

Round 1: Mr6sc
Round 2: 6inc
Round 3: (sc, inc) repeat 6 times
Round 4: (sc, inc, 1 sc) repeat 6 times
Round 5: (3sc, inc) repeat 6 times
Round 6-7: 30sc
Round 8: (2sc, inc) repeat 3 times, 12sc, (inc, 2sc) repeat 3 times
Round 9: 36sc
Round 10: (2sc, inc) repeat 4 times, 12sc, (inc, 2sc) repeat 4 times
Round 11: 44sc
Round 12: (2sc, dec) repeat 4 times, 12 sc, (dec, 2sc) repeat 4 times
Round 13: (2sc, dec, 2sc) repeat 6 times
Round 14: (3sc, dec) repeat 6 times
Round 15: (2sc, dec) repeat 6 times

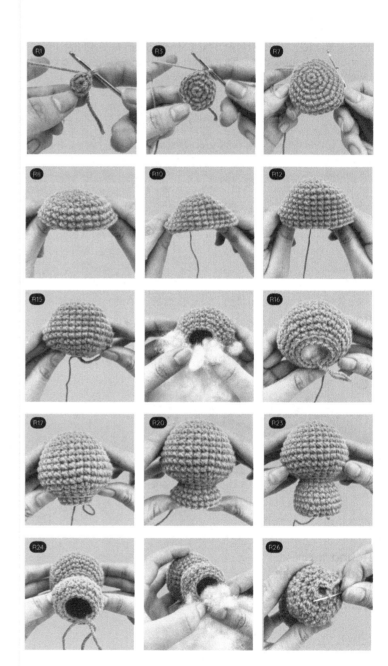

- NOTE

Stuff until full

Round 16: BLO18sc
Round 17: 18sc
Round 18: (sc, inc, sc) repeat 6 times
Round 19-20: 24sc
Round 21: (3sc, inc) repeat 6 times
Round 22: 30sc
Round 23: (3sc, dec) repeat 6 times
Round 24: (2sc, dec) repeat 6 times

- NOTE

Stuff until full

Round 25: (sc, dec) repeat 6 times
Round 26: 6dec

Mouth

Round1: 6ch, work into the 2nd st
sc , 2hdc, sc, w, 3 sc, inc
Round 2: 12sc

<u>Use Black thread to sew the mouth</u>

Towel

Round 1: Work into the 16th stitch, with 4dc per stitch

Finish

- Attach the safety eyes and mouth to the head.
- Attach the arms and legs to the body.
- Sew the mouth and nose by Black thread.

SCAN ME
▼

Simon The Tiger

(Difficult level 🧶 🧶 🧶 🧶)

Little Simon, the tiger cub, was always curious about everything around him and often ventured into the forest to play. His father constantly forbade him from going too deep, fearing he would get lost, but Simon never listened. After getting stuck in the forest overnight, his father was furious and grounded him from playing outside for a whole month! Oh my gosh!

Materials

- Yarns (milk cotton): white, yellow, brown
- Thread: Brown
- Stuffing
- Safety eyes: 6mm
- Crochet hook 4.

Size
Approximately 2.7 inches wide by 4.7 inches tall

Skills
Magic ring (14), Single Crochet (15), Increase (17), Decrease (17), Changing Colors, Chain (15), Front Loop Only (18)

Arms

Start with brown yarn
Round 1: Mr6sc

Change to yellow yarn
Round 2-5: 6sc

Make 2 pieces

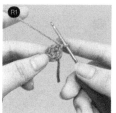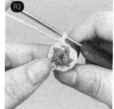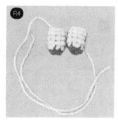

Legs

Start with brown yarn
Round 1: Mr6sc

Change to yellow yarn
Round 2: (sc, inc) repeat 3 times
Round 3-4: 9sc

Fasten off, leave long yarn for sewing

Ears

Round 1: Mr6sc
Round 2: 6inc
Round 3: 12sc

Fasten off, leave long yarn for sewing

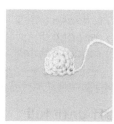

Head and body

Round 1: Mr6sc
Round 2: 6inc
Round 3: (sc, inc) repeat 6 times
Round 4: (2sc, inc) repeat 6 times
Round 5: (3sc, inc) repeat 6 times
Round 6: 30sc
Round 7: (4sc, inc) repeat 6 times
Round 8-10: 36sc
Round 11: 9sc, (sc, inc) repeat 3 times, 6sc, (inc, sc) repeat 3 times, 9sc
Round 12-13: 42sc
Round 14: 9sc, (sc, dec) repeat 3 times, 6sc, (dec, sc) repeat 3 times, 9sc
Round 15: (4sc, dec) repeat 6 times
Round 16: (3sc, dec) repeat 6 times
Round 17: (2sc, dec) repeat 6 times

NOTE

Stuff until full

Start to crochet body
Round 18: FLO (2sc, inc) repeat 6 times
Round 19: (3sc, inc) repeat 6 times
Round 20: (4sc, inc) repeat 6 times
Round 21-26: 36sc
Round 27: (4sc, dec) repeat 6 times
Round 28: (3sc, dec) repeat 6 times
Round 29: (2sc, dec) repeat 6 times

NOTE

Stuff until full

Round 30: (sc, dec) repeat 6 times
Round 31: 6dec

Fasten off

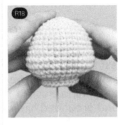

Muzzles

Round 1: Mr6sc
Round 2: Slst

Cut the yarn

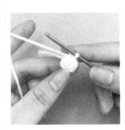

Collar

30ch, continue crocheting from 3ch from hook: DC3TOG repeat 27 times

<u>1ch, Fasten off, leave long yarn for sewing</u>

Finish

- Sew the ears to the head between round 3 and round 7.
- Sew the muzzles to the head.
- Sew the nose and eyebrows by Brown thread.
- Attach the arms to the body.
- Sew the legs to the body.
- Insert safety eyes between R9 and R10 at the distance of 6 st from each other.
- Wear the collar.

SCAN ME

Aqua The Blue Whale

Difficult level

One serene morning, a kind fisherman named Leo spotted Aqua while casting his nets. Instead of capturing her, Leo marveled at her beauty and they shared a moment of understanding. From that day on, Leo would often see Aqua, and they became silent friends, bound by the whispering waves.

Materials
- Yarns (milk cotton): blue
- Thread: Black
- Stuffing
- Safety eyes: 8mm
- Crochet hook 4.

Size
Approximately 4 inches wide by 6.3 inches tall

Skills
Magic ring (14), Single Crochet (15), Increase (17), Decrease (17)

Body

Round 1: Mr6sc
Round 2: 6inc (12)
Round 3: (sc, inc) repeat 6 times (18)
Round 4: (2sc, inc) repeat 6 times (24)
Round 5: (3sc, inc) repeat 6 times (30)
Round 6: (4sc, inc) repeat 6 times (36)
Round 7: (5sc, inc) repeat 6 times (42)
Round 8: (6sc, inc) repeat 6 times (48)
Round 9: (7sc, inc) repeat 6 times (54)
Round 10: (8sc, inc)repeat 6 times (60)
Round 11-22: 60sc
Round 23: (8sc, dec) repeat 6 times (54)
Round 24: (7sc, dec) repeat 6 times (48)
Round 25: dec, sc, dec, sc, dec, 32sc, dec, sc, dec, sc, dec (42)
Round 26: 42sc
Round 27: dec, sc, dec, sc, dec, 26sc, dec, sc, dec, sc, dec (36)
Round 28: 36sc
Round 29: 3dec, 24sc, 3dec (30)
Round 30: 30sc
Round 31: 2dec, 22sc, 2dec (26)
Round 32: 26sc

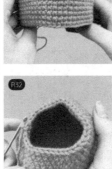

NOTE
Stuff until full

Round 33: dec, 22sc, dec (24)
Round 34: dec, 20sc, dec (22)
Round 35: dec, 8sc, 2dec, 6sc, dec (18)
Round 36: 2dec, 10sc, 2dec (14)

> **┌─ NOTE ─────────────────┐**
>
> **Stuff until full**

Round 37: 6sc, dec, sc, dec, 3sc (12)
Round 38: 5sc, dec, sc, dec, 2sc (10)
Round 39: sc, inc, 4sc, dec, 2sc (10)
Round 40: 10sc
Round 41: 10inc (20)
Round 42: 20sc

> **┌─ NOTE ─────────────────┐**
>
> **To crochet the tail: divide it into two fin sections, with each fin being 10sc**

SECTION 1
Round 43-45: 10sc
Round 46: 5dec

Cut the yarn

SECTION 2
Round 43-44: 10sc
Round 45: 5dec

Cut the yarn

  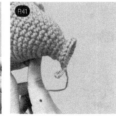

Fins

> **┌─ NOTE ─────────────────┐**
>
> **This part is not stuffed**

Round 1: Mr6sc (6)
Round 2: (sc, inc) repeat 3 times (9)
Round 3: (2sc, inc) repeat 3 times (12)
Round 4: (3sc, inc) repeat 3 times (15)
Round 5: 15sc
Round 6: (3sc, dec) repeat 3 times (12)
Round 7: 12sc
Round 8: (sc, dec) repeat 4 times (8)
Round 9: 8sc
Round 10: 4dec (4)

Sew it closed and cut the yarn, leaving a long tail for sewing

  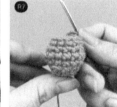

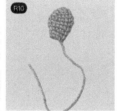  

Finish

- Attach the eyes to the body.
- Attach the fins to the body.

SCAN ME

Bambam The Giraffe

(Difficult level)

The giraffe Bambam, with his long neck, was busy munching on some leaves when suddenly, he felt an itch in his nose and sneezed loudly. The powerful sneeze caused Bambam's head to bump into a bird's nest high in the tree, making leaves scatter all over the ground.

Materials

- Yarns (milk cotton): white, yellow, brown
- Thread: Black
- Stuffing
- Safety eyes: 6mm
- Crochet hook 4.

Size

Approximately 2 inches wide by 6 inches tall

Skills

Magic ring (14), Single Crochet (15), Increase (17), Decrease (17), Changing Colors, Slip Stitch (19)

Head

Round 1: Mr6sc
Round 2: (inc) repeat 6 times
Round 3: (sc, inc) repeat 6 times
Round 4: (2sc, inc) repeat 6 times
Round 5: (3sc, inc) repeat 6 times
Round 6: (4sc, inc) repeat 6 times
Round 7-14: 36 sc
Round 15: (4sc, dec) repeat 6 times
Round 16: (3sc, dec) repeat 6 times
Round 17: (2sc, dec) repeat 6 times

- NOTE -

Stuff until full

Round 18: (sc, dec) repeat 6 times

Fasten off and leave a long tail for sewing.

 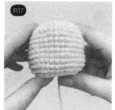 

Ears

Round 1: Mr5sc (5)
Round 2: 2sc, inc, 2 sc (6)
Round 3: 6inc (12)
Round 4-8: 12sc

Fasten off and leave a long tail for sewing
Fold the ear edges together and sew them together

 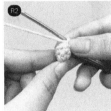 

Horn

Start with brown yarn
Round 1: Mr8sc
Round 2-3: 8sc

Change to yellow yarn
Round 4: 3sc, dec, 3sc
Round 5-7: 7sc

Stuff the brown part of the horn.
Fasten off and leave a long tail for sewing

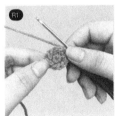 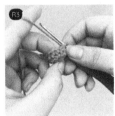 

Arms

Start with brown yarn
Round 1: Mr6sc
Round 2: (sc, inc) repeat 3 times
Round 3: 9sc

Change to yellow yarn
Round 4-10: 9sc

Stuff the brown part of the arm
Fold the top opening flat and 3sc through both sides
Fasten off and leave a long tail for sewing

Muzzles

Start with white yarn

Round 1: Mr6sc (6)
Round 2: (inc) repeat 6 times
Round 3: (3sc, inc) repeat 3 times
Round 4: 15sc

Fasten off and leave a long tail for sewing.

 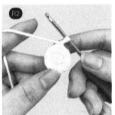 

Spots

Make 3 pieces
Start with brown yarn

Round 1: Mr8sc

Fasten off and leave a long tail for sewing.

 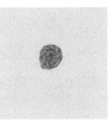

Legs and body

Start with brown yarn

Round 1: Mr6sc
Round 2: sc, 5inc
Round 3: 11sc

Change to yellow yarn

Round 4-7: 11sc

Fasten off.
Crochet the second leg, do not fasten off

Connect 2 legs: Make 1 ch on the second leg and join with the first leg.

Round 8: 11sc on the first leg, inc in 1ch, 11sc on the second leg, inc in 1ch (opposite side)
Round 9-14: 24sc
Round 15: Make dec on the sides of body
Round 16-18: 24sc
Round 19: (2sc, dec) repeat 6 times
Round 20: (sc, dec) repeat 6 times

NOTE

Stuff until full

Round 21-23: 12sc

Fasten off

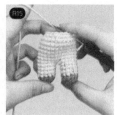

Finish

- Sew the nose on the muzzle by Black thread.
- Sew the arms to the body.
- Connect the body and head.
- Insert safety eyes between R9 and R10 at the distance of 6 st from each other.
- Attach the safety eyes, muzzle, horns and ears to the head.
- Attach the spots to the body.
- Sew the arms to the body.

SCAN ME

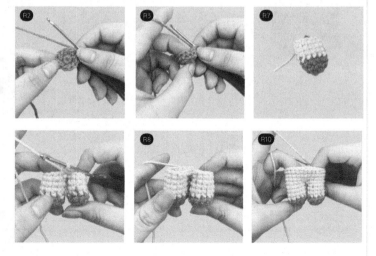

Huff The Lion

(Difficult level 🧶 🧶 🧶 🧶)

One day, while he was fuming with anger, Huff accidentally tripped over a rock and tumbled down the hill, ending in a spectacular but hilarious somersault. When he stood up, covered in grass and flowers, the forest animals couldn't hold back their laughter, and Huff himself couldn't stay grumpy for long. For the first time, a bright smile appeared on the face of the grumpiest lion in the forest.

Materials

- Yarns (milk cotton): yellow, brown
- Thread: Brown
- Stuffing
- Safety eyes: 8mm
- Nose: 5mm
- Crochet hook 4.

Size
Approximately 2.7 inches wide by 4.8 inches tall

Skills
Magic ring (14), Single Crochet (15), Increase (17), Decrease (17) , Loop, Chain (15), Skip (19), Double Treble Crochet (22), Double Crochet (21)

Arms

Round 1: Mr6sc
Round 2-6: 6sc

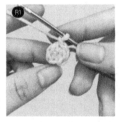  

Ears

Round 1: Mr6sc
Round 2: (sc, inc) repeat 3 times

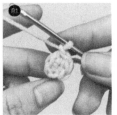  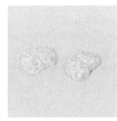

Mane

Round 1: 56ch loop around the end of each leg to form a circle
Round 2: (sc, sk, 5dc, sk, sc, 2sk, 5E, 2sk) repeat 5 times, sk, 2sk, 5e, 2sk

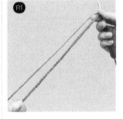 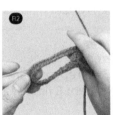 

Legs + Body + Head

Round 1: Mr6sc
Round 2: (sc, inc) repeat 5 times
Round 3: (sc, inc) repeat 6 times
4ch, connect 2 legs
Round 4: 8sc, 4sc, 8sc, 4sc
Round 5-9: 24sc
Round 10: (2sc, dec) repeat 6 times
Round 11: Connect 2 arms: 3sc (body), 6sc (arm), 9sc (body), 6sc (arm), 6sc (body)

— NOTE —

Stuff until full

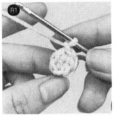
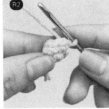

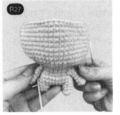

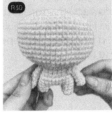

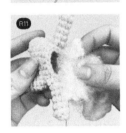

Round 12: (3sc, dec) repeat 6 times
Round 13: (sc, dec, sc) repeat 6 times
Round 14: 18sc
Round 15: 18sc
Round 16: (5sc, inc) repeat 6 times
Round 17: (3sc, inc, 3sc) repeat 6 times
Round 18: (5sc, inc) repeat 8 times
Round 19-27: 56sc
Round 28: (5sc, dec) repeat 8 times
Round 29: (3sc, dec, 3sc) repeat 6 times
Round 30: (5sc, dec) repeat 6 times
Round 31: (4sc, dec) repeat 6 times
Round 32: (3sc, dec) repeat 6 times
Round 33: (sc, dec, sc) repeat 6 times

— NOTE —

Stuff until full

Round 34: (sc, dec) repeat 6 times

Finish

- Sew the arms to the body
- Connect the body and head: Sew on the inside
- Sew the mouth and eyebrows by Brown thread.
- Attach the safety eyes and nose, ears to the head.
- Wear the mane.

SCAN ME

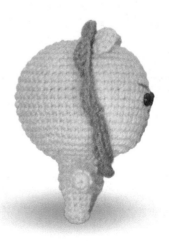

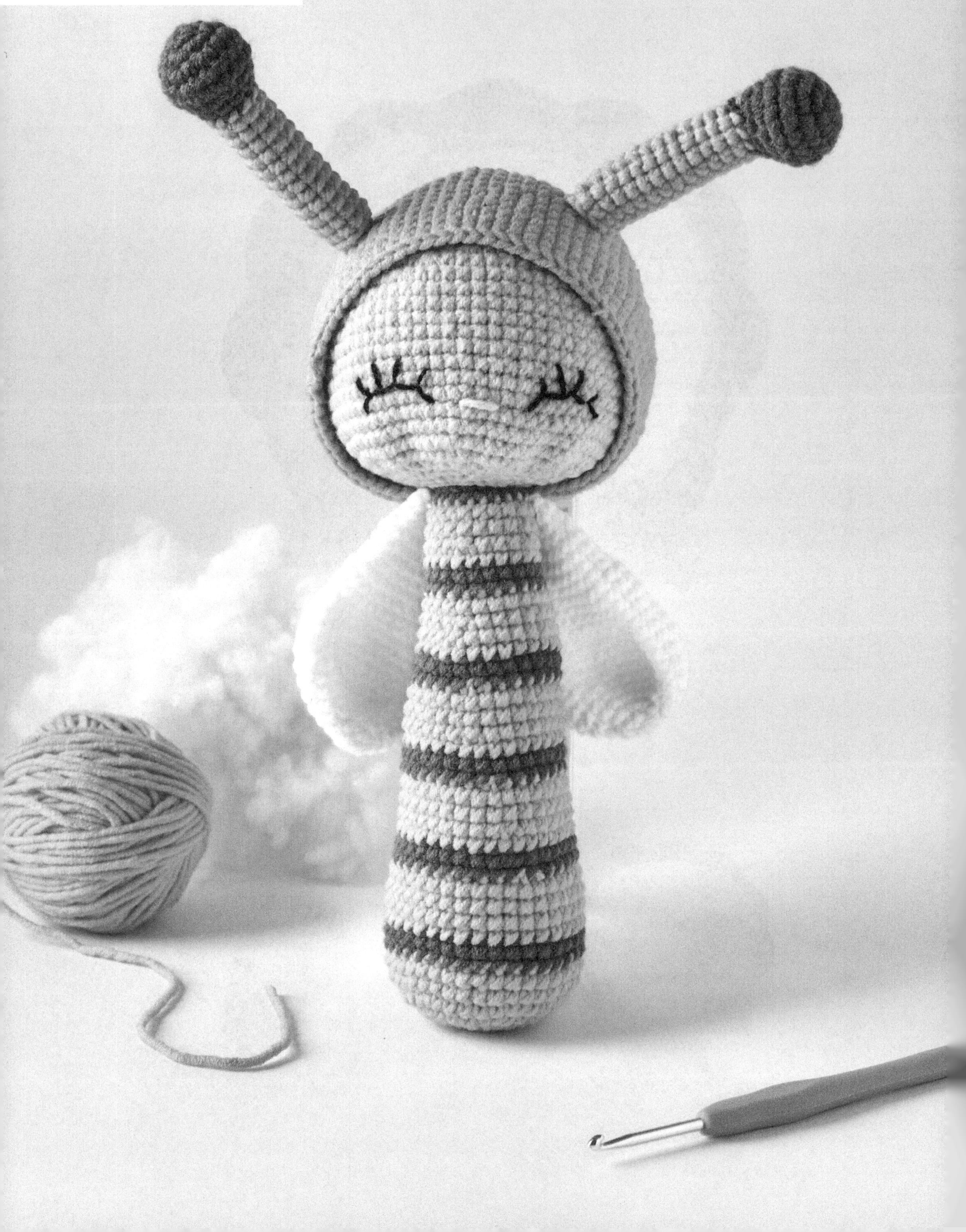

Mia The Bee

Difficult level

Mia always spent time caring for flowers and listening to love stories from the older bees. One day, she met Max, a mischievous bee from another hive. Max liked to tease Mia, which initially made her annoyed. However, over time, Mia found herself drawn to Max's lively personality and sense of humor...

Materials
- Yarns (milk cotton): yellow, grey, brown, white
- Thread: Black, Skin
- Stuffing
- Crochet hook 4.

Size
Approximately 4 inches wide by 10 inches tall

Skills
Magic ring (14), Single Crochet (15), Increase (17), Decrease (17), 3 Single Crochet Together (16), Chain (15), Changing colors

Head

Round 1: Mr6sc
Round 2: 6inc (12)
Round 3: (sc, inc) repeat 6 times (18)
Round 4: (2sc, inc) repeat 6 times (24)
Round 5: (3sc, inc) repeat 6 times (30)
Round 6: (4sc, inc) repeat 6 times (36)
Round 7: (5sc, inc) repeat 6 times (42)
Round 8: (6sc, inc) repeat 6 times (48)
Round 9: (7sc, inc) repeat 6 times (54)
Round 10: 54sc
Round 11: (8sc, inc) repeat 6 times (60)
Round 12: (9sc, inc) repeat 6 times (66)
Round 13-24: 66sc
Round 25: (dec, 9sc) repeat 6 times (60)
Round 26: 30dec (30)
Round 27: (dec, 3sc) repeat 6 times (24)
Round 28: (dec, 2sc) repeat 6 times (18)

<u>Tie off and cut the yarn.</u>

NOTE

Stuff until full

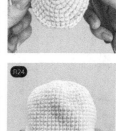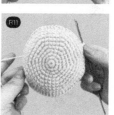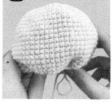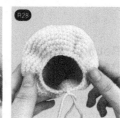

Whiskers

Start with brown yarn

Round 1: Mr6sc
Round 2: 6inc (12)
Round 3: (sc, inc) repeat 6 times (18)
Round 4-5: 18sc
Round 6: (sc, dec) repeat 6 times (12)
Round 7: (4sc, dec) repeat 2 times (10)

Change to yellow yarn

Round 8-20: 10sc

Tie a knot and leave a long tail for sewing later

Hat

Round 1: Mr6sc
Round 2: 6inc (12)
Round 3: (sc, inc) repeat 6 times (18)
Round 4: (2sc, inc) repeat 6 times (24)
Round 5: (3sc, inc) repeat 6 times (30)
Round 6: (4sc, inc) repeat 6 times (36)
Round 7: (5sc, inc) repeat 6 times (42)
Round 8: (6sc, inc) repeat 6 times (48)
Round 9: (7sc, inc) repeat 6 times (54)
Round 10: (8sc, inc) repeat 6 times (60)
Round 11: (9sc, inc) repeat 6 times (66)
Round 12-26: 66sc

Tie a knot and leave a long tail for sewing later

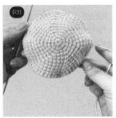

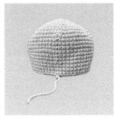

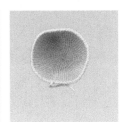

Body

Round 1: Mr6sc
Round 2: 6inc (12)
Round 3: (sc, inc) repeat 6 times (18)
Round 4: (2sc, inc) repeat 6 times (24)
Round 5: (3sc, inc) repeat 6 times (30)
Round 6: (4sc, inc) repeat 6 times (36)
Round 7-8: 36sc

Next, alternate crocheting 2 rounds of brown yarn with 4 rounds of yellow yarn.

Round 9-14: 36sc
Round 15: (16sc, dec) repeat 2 times (34)
Round 16-17: 34sc
Round 18: (15sc, dec) repeat 2 times (32)
Round 19-20: 32sc
Round 21: (14sc, dec) repeat 2 times (30)
Round 22-23: 30sc
Round 24: (13sc, dec) repeat 2 times (28)
Round 25-26: 28sc
Round 27: (12sc, dec) repeat 2 times (26)
Round 28-29: 26sc
Round 30: (11sc, dec) repeat 2 times (24)
Round 31-32: 24sc

Round 33: (10sc, dec) repeat 2 times (22)
Round 34-35: 22sc
Round 36: (9sc, dec) repeat 2 times (20)
Round 37-38: 20sc
Round 39: (8sc, dec) repeat 2 times (18)
Round 40: 18sc

NOTE

Stuff until full

Wings

Round 1: Mr6sc
Round 2: (sc, inc) repeat 3 times (9)
Round 3: 9 inc (18)
Round 4: 18sc
Round 5: (2sc, inc) repeat 6 times (24)
Round 6: 24sc
Round 7: (3sc, inc) repeat 6 times (30)
Round 8-11: 30sc
Round 12: (dec, 3sc) repeat 6 times (24)
Round 13-15: 24sc
Round 16: (dec, 2sc) repeat 6 times (18)
Round 17-19: 18sc
Round 20: (dec, sc) repeat 6 times (12)
Round 21-22: 12sc

Fold the wings in half, crochet through both edges. Fasten off, leaving a long tail for sewing.

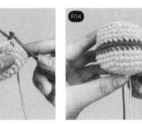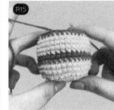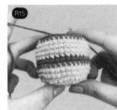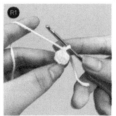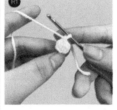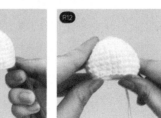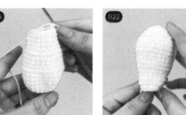

Finish

- Sew the Wings to the body.
- **Connect the body and head:** Sew on the inside
- Sew the nose by Skin thread
- Skip 2 stitches to both sides to sew the eyes.

SCAN ME
▼

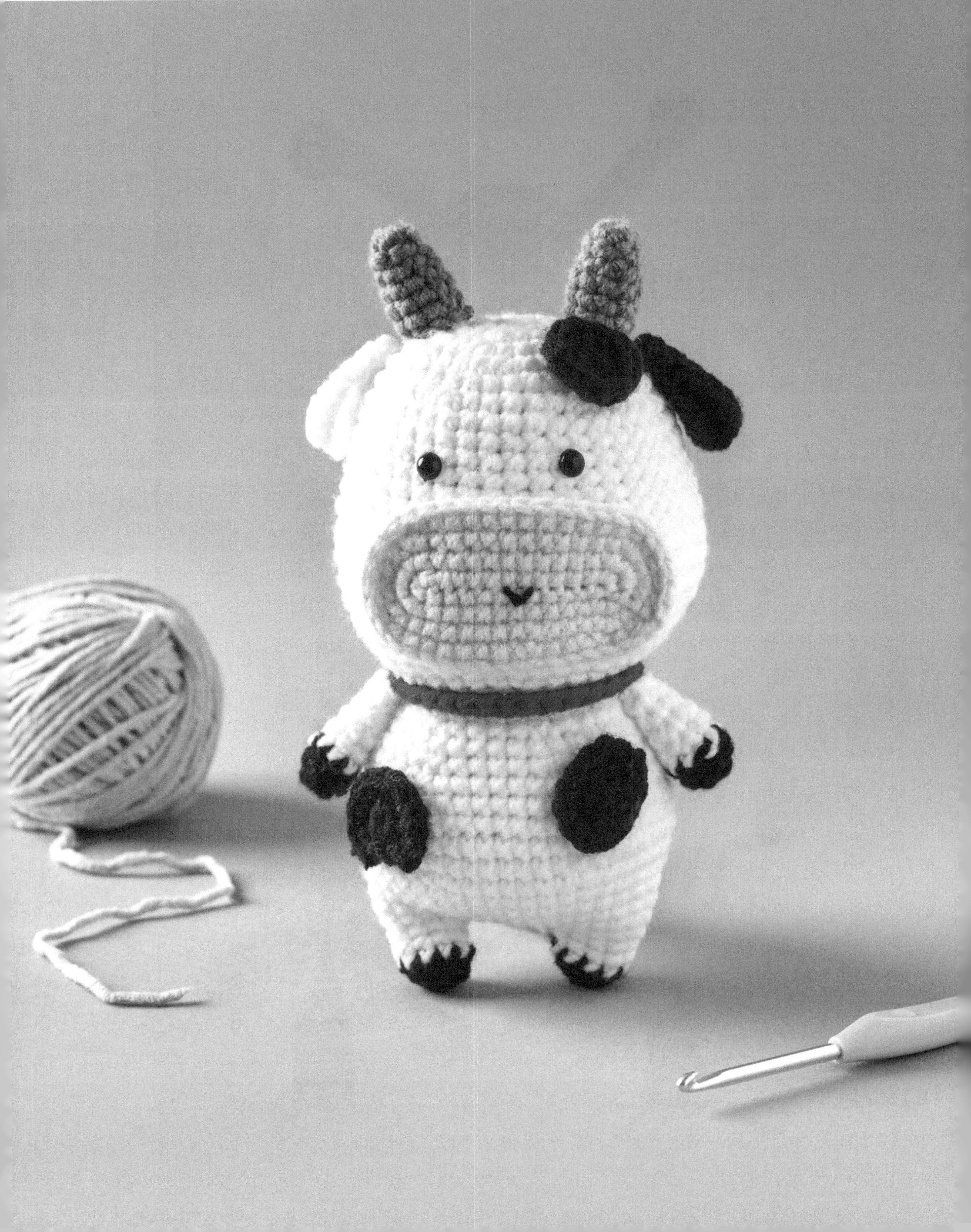

Coco The Dairy Cow

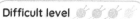

(Difficult level)

Coco the Cow lives on a sprawling farm with a kind-hearted elderly couple. Every day, she gives milk to the farmer's wife and enjoys peaceful strolls up the hill with the farmer. Coco absolutely adores the red scarf that the farmer's wife lovingly knitted for her, and she wears it around her neck wherever she goes.

Materials
- Yarns (milk cotton): black, white, skin color, brown, red
- Stuffing
- Thread: Black
- Safety eyes: 6mm
- Crochet hook 4.

Size
Approximately 3.5 inches wide by 6.5 inches tall

Skills
Magic ring (14), Single Crochet (15), Increase (17), Decrease (17), 3 Single Crochet Together (16), Changing colors

Legs and body

<u>Start with black yarn</u>
Round 1: Mr6sc
Round 2: (sc, inc) repeat 3 times

<u>Change to white yarn</u>
Round 3-4: 9sc
Matching 2 legs by 6ch
Round 5: 30sc
Round 6: (4sc, inc) repeat 6 times
Round 7: sc, inc, 24sc, (inc, sc) repeat 5 times
Round 8-10: 42sc
Round 11: (6sc, inc) repeat 6 times
Round 12-14: 48sc
Round 15: (6sc, dec) repeat 6 times
Round 16: 42sc
Round 17: (5sc, dec) repeat 6 times
Round 18: 36sc
Round 19: (4sc, dec) repeat 6 times
Round 20: 30sc

 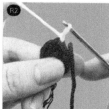 
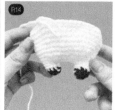  
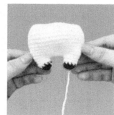

NOTE
Stuff until full

Horns

Round 1: Mr6sc
Round 2: 6sc
Round 3: (sc, inc) repeat 3 times
Round 4-6: 9sc

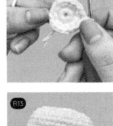

> **- NOTE -**
>
> **Stuff until full**

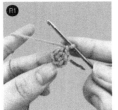
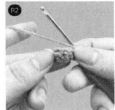
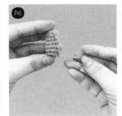

Head

Round 1: Mr8sc
Round 2: 8inc
Round 3: (sc, inc) repeat 8 times
Round 4: (3sc, inc) repeat 6 times
Round 5: 2sc, inc, (4sc, inc) repeat 5 times, 2sc
Round 6: 36sc
Round 7: (5sc, inc) repeat 6 times
Round 8-13: 42sc
Round 14: 4sc, inc, (2sc, inc) repeat 11 times, 4sc
Round 15-18: 54sc
Round 19: (7sc, dec) repeat 6 times

> **- NOTE -**
>
> **Stuff until full**

Round 20: (6sc, dec) repeat 6 times
Round 21: (5sc, dec) repeat 6 times
Round 22: (4sc, dec) repeat 6 times

Connect the body and head: Sew on the inside

Mouth

Round 1: 12ch, 10sc, w, 9sc, inc
Round 2: inc, 10sc, 3inc, 10sc, 2inc
Round 3: sc, inc, 10sc, (sc, inc) repeat 3 times, 10sc, (sc, inc) repeat 2 times
Round 4: 38sc

Sew the mouth by black thread

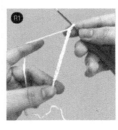

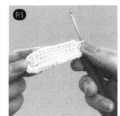

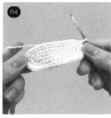
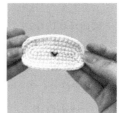

Arms

Round 1: Mr6sc
Round 2: (2sc, inc) repeat 2 times
<u>Change to white yarn</u>
Round 3-4: 8sc
Round 5: (sc, dec) repeat 2 times, 2sc
Round 6: 6sc

  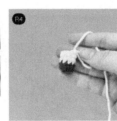

Ears

<u>Make 2 pieces (black and white)</u>
Round 1: Mr6sc
Round 2: 6 inc
Round 3: (sc, inc) repeat 6 times

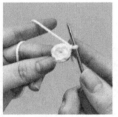 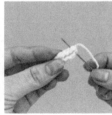 

Scarf

Chain a number of sts to fit the necklace, crochet 1 row of single crochet (sc)

Black spot 1

Round 1: Mr8sc
Round 2: 8inc

Black spot 2

Round 1: 5ch
Round 2: 3sc, w, 2sc, inc
Round 3: sc, inc, 2sc, 3inc, 2sc, sc, inc

Black spot 3

Round 1: Mr8sc
Round 2: 8inc without joining

  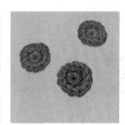

Finish

- Attach the safety eyes and horns to the head.
- Sew the 2 arms and 2 legs onto the body.

SCAN ME

Bubu The Corgi

(**Difficult level** 🧶🧶🧶🧶)

Sarah took her chubby Corgi, Bubu, for a walk. Bubu spotted a wallet left behind by a food truck and quickly grabbed it in his mouth, bringing it back to Sarah. Thanks to Bubu, Sarah was able to return the wallet to its owner, and Bubu was rewarded with a giant piece of beef from the grateful man!

Materials

- Yarns (milk cotton): white, yellow
- Thread: Brown
- Stuffing
- Safety eyes: 8mm
- Crochet hook 4.

Size
Approximately 2 inches wide by 3.5 inches tall

Skills
Magic ring (14), Single Crochet (15), Increase (17), Decrease (17), Changing Colors, Single Crochet 3 Together (16), Slip Stitch (19), Skip (19), Loop

Legs

Make 4 pieces

Round 1: Mr6sc
Round 2: 6sc
Round 3: sc, (sc, inc) repeat 2 times, sc

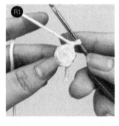 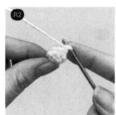 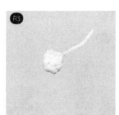

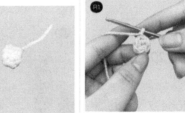

Ears

Start with yellow yarn

Round 1: Mr6sc
Round 2: inc, sc, inc, (white) 2sc, (yellow) inc (9)
Round 3: (yellow) inc, 2sc, inc, sc, (white) sc, inc, (yellow) 2sc (12)

Round 4: (yellow) 7sc, (white) 4sc, (yellow) sc (12)
Round 5: (yellow) 3sc, inc, 3sc, (white) inc, 3sc, (yellow) inc (15)
Round 6: 15sc (yellow)

Cut the yarn and leave a long tail for sewing.

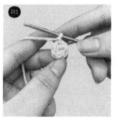 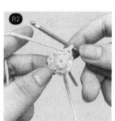 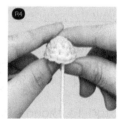

Nose

Round 1: Mr6sc
Round 2: 6inc
Round 3: (3sc, inc) repeat 3 times (15)
Round 4: (4sc, inc) repeat 3 times

Cut the yarn

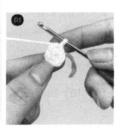 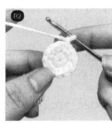 

Body and Head

Connect the legs

Round 1: 6ch, 4sc start on the 2nd ch, 3sc in 1, 3sc, inc (12)
Round 2: inc, 3sc, 3inc, 3sc, 2inc (18)
Round 3: sc, inc, 3sc, (sc, inc) repeat 3 times, 3sc, (sc, inc) repeat 2 times (24)
Round 4: sc, inc, 4sc, (sc, inc, sc) repeat 3 times, 3sc, (sc, inc, sc) repeat 2 times (30)
Round 5: connect 4 legs
(Start from 2nd st, end at 6th st on leg)
- sc, (sc, inc, sc) repeat 2 times work on leg, sk2, 5sc, connect 1st leg
- (sc, inc, sc) repeat 2 times work on leg, sk2, 6sc, connect 2nd leg
- (sc, inc, sc) repeat 2 times work on leg, sk2, 5sc, connect 3rd leg
- (sc, inc, dc) repeat 2 times work on leg, sk2, 5sc, connect 4th leg

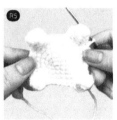  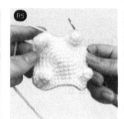

Sew the skipped stitches for legs

Round 6: inc, 48sc, 2inc, 2sc, inc (58)
Round 7: (white) 8sc, 8sc (yellow), (white) 20sc, 8sc (yellow), 14sc (58)

Start to change to yellow yarn when done 7 white sts, 2 white loop on the hook

Done 8th white sts, yellow yarn on the hook

Round 8: (white) 8sc, (yellow) 9sc, (white) 18sc, (yellow) 9sc, (white) 14sc (58)
Round 9: (white) 7sc, (yellow) 10sc, (white) 18sc, (yellow) 10sc, (white) 9sc, (yellow) 3sc, (white) sc (58)
Round 10: (white) 7sc, (yellow) 10sc, (white) 18sc, (yellow) 10sc, (white) 9sc, (yellow) 4sc (58)
Round 11: (yellow) sc, (white) sc, dec, 2sc, (yellow) 11sc, (white) 18sc, (yellow) 11sc, (white) 2sc, dec, 2sc, (yellow) dec, 2sc, dec (54)
Round 12: (yellow) sc, dec, 13sc, (white) 18sc, (yellow) 14sc, (yellow) (dec, dec) repeat 2 times (51)
Round 13: (yellow) dec, 2sc, dec, 9sc, (white) 18sc, (yellow) 9sc, dec, 2sc, dec, 3sc (47)

Round 14: (yellow) 4sc, dec, 7sc, (white) 3sc, dec, 8sc, dec, 3sc, (yellow) 7sc, dec, 4sc, SC3TOG (41)
Round 15: (yellow) 2dec, 8sc, (white) 3sc, inc, 8sc, inc, 3sc, (yellow) 8sc, 2dec, sc (39)
Round 16: (yellow) 2dec, 6sc, (white) 5sc, (sc, inc) repeat 4 times, 5sc, (yellow) 6sc, 2dec, sc (39)
Round 17: (yellow) 9sc, (white) 20sc, (yellow) 8sc, dec (38)
Round 18: (yellow) (inc, sc) repeat 3 times, 6sc, (white) 18sc, (yellow) 6sc, (sc, inc) repeat 2 times (42)
Round 19: (yellow) 15sc, 2dec, (white) 4sc, (yellow) 2dec, 15sc (38)
Round 20-23: (yellow) 18sc, (white) 2sc, (yellow) 18sc (38)
Round 24: (yellow) 18sc, (white) dec, (yellow) 16sc, dec (36)

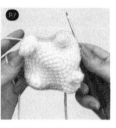  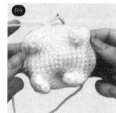

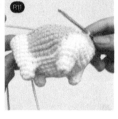 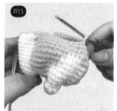 

Change to yellow yarn

Round 25: (sc, dec, sc) repeat 9 times (27)

> **NOTE**
> **Stuff until full**

Round 26: (sc, dec) repeat 9 times (18)
Round 27: 9dec (9)
Round 28: sc, 4dec (5)

Cut the yarn and fasten off

NOTE

*Make the butt shape: By threading the yarn down through the button and collar, tightening it until achieving the desired curve.

Finish

- Sew the nose by Brown thread.
- Attach the safety eyes, nose and ears to the head.

SCAN ME

Nana The Monkey

(Difficult level 🧶 🧶 🧶)

Nana sat sadly on the tree branch. Her favorite banana tree had no more bananas left. Feeling down, Nana spotted a bunch of ripe bananas hidden among the leaves. She jumped up joyfully and ate them, her sadness disappearing instantly.

Materials

- Yarns (milk cotton): skin, brown, blue
- Thread: Black
- Stuffing
- Safety eyes: 6mm
- Crochet hook 4.

Size

Approximately 3 inches wide by 5 inches tall

Skills

Magic ring (14), Single Crochet (15), Increase (17), Decrease (17), Changing colors, Double Treble Crochet (22), Double Crochet (21), Half Double Crochet (20).

Head

Round 1: Mr6sc
Round 2: 6inc
Round 3: (sc, inc) repeat 6 times
Round 4: (sc, inc, sc) repeat 6 times
Round 5: (3sc, inc) repeat 6 times
Round 6: (2sc, inc, 2sc) repeat 6 times
Round 7: (5sc, inc) repeat 6 times
Round 8: (3sc, inc, 3sc) repeat 6 times
Round 9: (7sc, inc) repeat 6 times
Round 10-17: 54sc
Round 18: (7sc, dec) repeat 6 times
Round 19: (3sc, dec, 3sc) repeat 6 times
Round 20: (5sc, dec) repeat 6 times
Round 21: (2sc, dec, 2sc) repeat 6 times
Round 22: (3sc, dec) repeat 6 times
Round 23: (sc, dec, sc) repeat 6 times

```
NOTE
 Cut the yarn and stuff until full
```

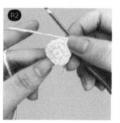 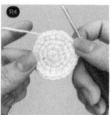 
 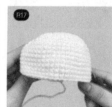 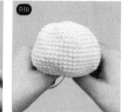

 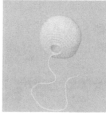

Ears (outside)

Round 1: Mr6sc
Round 2: 6inc
Round 3: sc, inc
Round 4: 18sc

 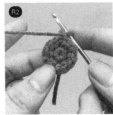 

Ears (inside)

Round 1: Mr6sc
Round 2: 6inc
<u>Cut the yarn</u>

Legs and body

<u>Make 2 pieces</u>

Round 1: Mr6sc
Round 2: 6inc
Round 3: 12sc
Round 4: (sc, inc) repeat 6 times
Round 5: 18sc

 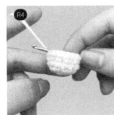 

NOTE

Connect 2 legs and body

Round 6: 18sc
Round 7-10: 36sc
Round 11: (2sc, dec, 2sc) repeat 6 times
Round 12-13: 30sc
Round 14: (3sc, dec) repeat 6 times
Round 15-16: 24sc
Round 17: (sc, dec, sc) repeat 6 times

NOTE

Stuff until full

  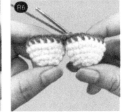

 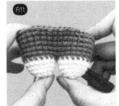 

Arms

Start with Skin yarn

Round 1: Mr7sc
Round 2: 7sc

Change to Brown yarn

Round 3 - 9: 7sc
Cut the yarn

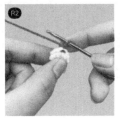

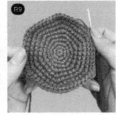

Towel

Round 1: 60ch
Round 2: 6sc

Finish

- **Connect the body and head:** Sew on the inside

- Sew the mouth and eyebrows by Black thread
- Attach the safety eyes
- Attach the hat to the head
- Attach the ears to the hat

Hat

Round 1: Mr6sc
Round 2: 6inc
Round 3: (sc, inc) repeat 6 times
Round 4: (sc, inc, sc) repeat 6 times
Round 5: (3sc, inc) repeat 6 times
Round 6: (2sc, inc, 2sc) repeat 6 times
Round 7: (5sc, inc) repeat 6 times
Round 8: (3sc, inc, 3sc) repeat 6 times
Round 9: (7sc, inc) repeat 6 times
Round 10-15: 54sc
Round 16: 13sc, 2hdc, 3dc, 2hdc, 7sc, 2hdc, 3dc, 2hdc, 7sc, 2hdc, 3dc, 2hdc, 12sc.
Round 17: 13sc, 3hdc, (dc, e, dc), 3hdc, 7sc, 3hdc, (dc, e, dc), 3hdc, 7sc, 3hdc, (dc, e, dc), 3hdc, 12sc

SCAN ME

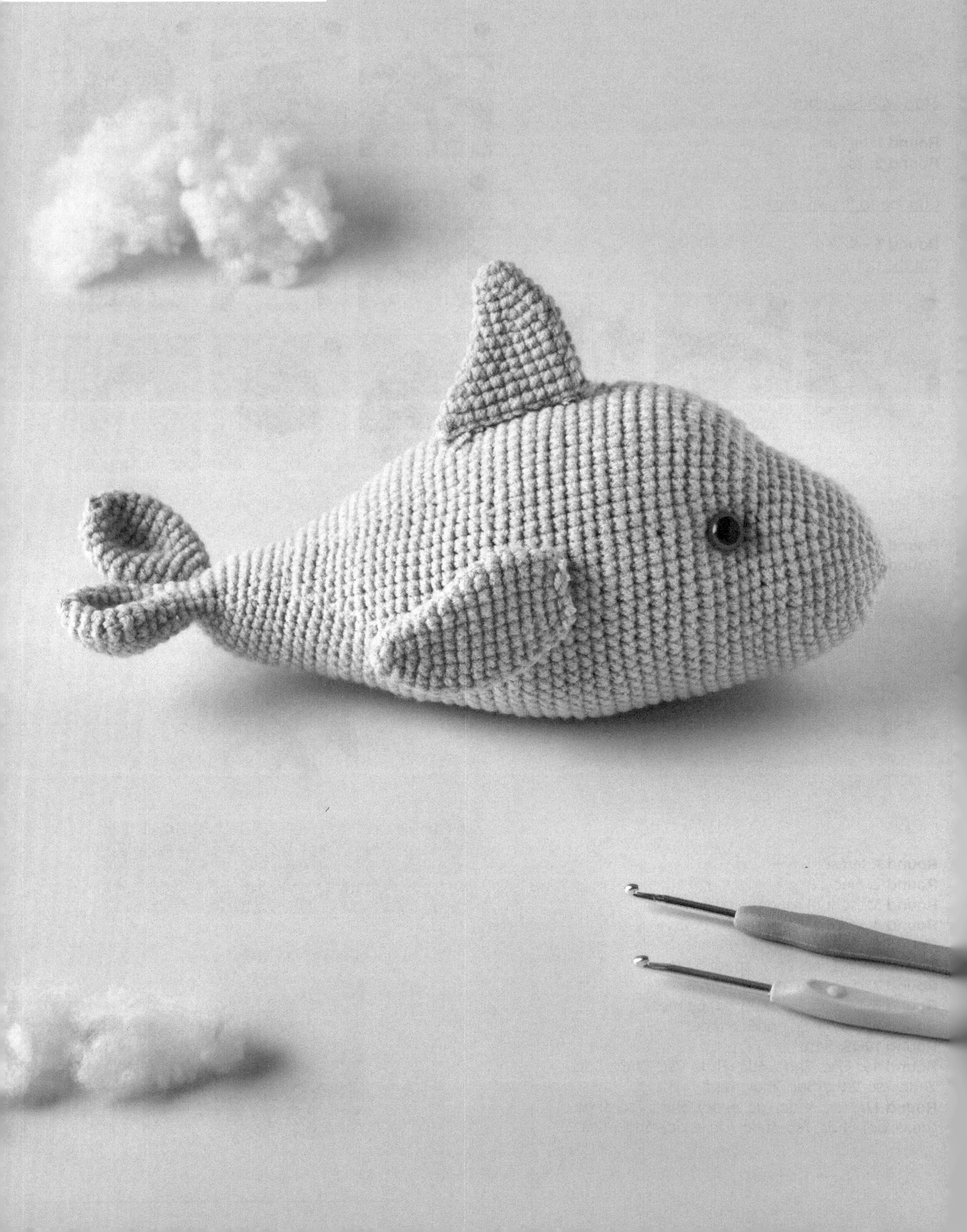

Aura The Dolphin

(Difficult level 🧶🧶🧶🧶)

One day, Aura noticed an old fisherman struggling to pull up his net, unaware that a large turtle was tangled in it. Swiftly, Aura swam over, skillfully using her nose to free the turtle and then led a large school of fish around the fisherman's boat.

Materials

- Yarns (milk cotton): blue
- Thread: Black
- Stuffing:
- Safety eyes: 8mm
- Crochet hook 4.

Size

Approximately 4 inches wide by 6.3 inches tall

Skills

Magic ring (14), Single Crochet (15), Increase (17), Decrease (17)

Head and body

Round 1: Mr6sc
Round 2: 6inc (12)
Round 3: (sc, inc) repeat 6 times (18)
Round 4: sc, inc, (2sc, inc) repeat 5 times, sc (24)
Round 5: (3sc, inc) repeat 6 times (30)
Round 6-7: 30sc (30)
Round 8: 2sc, inc, (4sc, inc) repeat 5 times, 2sc (36)
Round 9: 36sc (36)
Round 10: (5sc, inc) repeat 6 times (42)
Round 11-13: 42sc (42)
Round 14: 15sc, 12inc, 15sc (54)
Round 15: 54sc (54)
Round 16: 4sc, inc, (8sc, inc) repeat 5 times, 4sc (60)
Round 17: 60sc (60)
Round 18: (9sc, inc) repeat 6 times (66)
Round 19: 66sc (66)
Round 20: 5sc, inc, (10sc, inc) repeat 5 times, 5sc (72)
Round 21-31: 72sc
Round 32: (10sc, dec) repeat 6 times (66)
Round 33: 66sc (66)
Round 34: 12sc, dec, (9sc, dec) repeat 4 times, 8sc (61)
Round 35-36: 61sc (61)

```
_NOTE_____

     Stuff until full
_____
```

Round 37: 12sc, dec, (8sc, dec) repeat 4 times, 7sc (56)
Round 38-39: 56sc (56)
Round 40: 12sc, dec, (7sc, dec) repeat 4 times, 6sc (51)
Round 41: 51sc (51)
Round 42: 12sc, dec, (6sc, dec) repeat 4 times, 5sc (46)
Round 43: 46sc (46)
Round 44: 12sc, dec, (5sc, dec) repeat 4 times, 4sc (41)
Round 45: 41sc (41)
Round 46: 12sc, dec, (4sc, dec) repeat 4 times, 3sc (36)
Round 47: 36sc (36)
Round 48: 12sc, dec, (3sc, dec) repeat 4 times, 2sc (31)
Round 49: 31sc (31)
Round 50: 12sc, dec, (2sc, dec) repeat 4 times, sc (26)
Round 51-53: 26sc (26)
Round 54: (11sc, dec) repeat 2 times (24)
Round 55: 24sc (24)
Round 56: (10sc, dec) repeat 2 times (22)

NOTE

Stuff until full

Round 57: (9sc, dec) repeat 2 times (20)
Round 58: 20sc (20)

Do not fasten off and continue to crochet the tail as per the pattern in the next section.

Tail

NOTE

Continue to crochet from R58 of the body, crochet as two separate tail fins

Continue to crochet from R58 of the body, crochet as two separate tail fins.
- Split R58 of the body into two parts
- Each part will have 10 stitches and will form one tail fin
- Do not cut off the yarn and continue to crochet in spiral
- Do not stuff the tail fins

FIRST TAIL FIN
Round 59: 10sc (10)
Round 60: (4sc, inc) repeat 2 times (12)
Round 61: (2sc, inc) repeat 4 times (16)
Round 62: 16sc (16)
Round 63: (3sc, inc) repeat 4 times (20)
Round 64: 20sc (20)
Round 65: (4sc, inc) repeat 4 times (24)
Round 66-67: 24sc (24)
Round 68: (4sc, dec) repeat 4 times (20)
Round 69: 20sc (20)
Round 70: (3sc, dec) repeat 4 times (16)
Round 71: (2sc, dec) repeat 4 times (12)
Round 72: 12sc (12)
Round 73: (sc, dec) repeat 4 times (8), close the hole with a needle and weave the yarn end in.

SECOND TAIL FIN
Go back to R58 and attach new yarn to the first stitch of the second part of r58
Continue to crochet R59 to R73 as per the pattern for the first tail fin

Back fin

Round 1: Mr6sc (6)
Round 2: (sc, inc) repeat 3 times (9)
Round 3: 9sc (9)
Round 4: (2sc, inc) repeat 3 times (12)
Round 5: (3sc, inc) repeat 3 times (15)
Round 6: 7sc, inc, 7sc (16)
Round 7: dec, 6sc, inc, 7sc (16)
Round 8: 7sc, 2inc, 7sc (18)
Round 9: 8sc, 2inc, 8sc (20)
Round 10: 9sc, 2inc, 9sc (22)
Round 11: 10sc, 2inc, 10sc (24)
Round 12: 11sc, 2inc, 11sc (26)
Round 13: 13sc, do not finish this round (13)

<u>Fasten off and leave a long tail for sewing; do not stuff.</u>

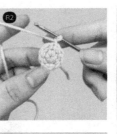 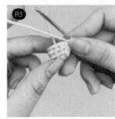 

 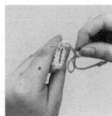 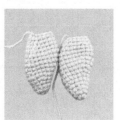

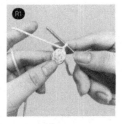 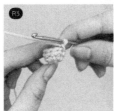 

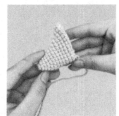

Finish

- Attach the safety eyes to the head: Tie or pinch at two points around the eyes to create an inward depression.
- Sew the fins to the body.

Side fins

Round 1: Mr6sc (6)
Round 2: (sc, inc) repeat 3 times (9)
Round 3: 9sc (9)
Round 4: (2sc, inc) repeat 3 times (12)
Round 5: (3sc, inc) repeat 3 times (15)
Round 6: 7sc, inc, 7sc (16)
Round 7: dec, 6sc, inc, 7sc (16)
Round 8: 7sc, 2inc, 7sc (18)
Round 9: 18sc (18)
Round 10: dec, 6sc, 2inc, 8sc (19)
Round 11: 19sc (19)
Round 12: dec, 17sc (18)
Round 13: dec, 16sc (17)
Round 14: dec, 5sc, dec, 6sc, dec (14)
Round 15: dec, 12sc (13)
<u>Fasten off and leave a long tail for sewing; do not stuff.</u>

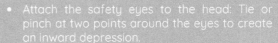

SCAN ME

Kitie The Cat

(**Difficult level** 🧶🧶🧶🧶)

In a small village, there was a wizard cat named Kitie, distinguished by its mysterious black and white fur. Kitie was not only intelligent but also knew how to cast spells, astonishing everyone in the village. One day, when the villagers were worried because pests were destroying their crops, Kitie used its magic to transform all the bugs into vibrant flowers.

Materials

- Yarns (milk cotton): white, black, orange
- Thread: Black
- Stuffing
- Safety eyes: 6mm
- Crochet hook 4.

Size
Approximately 3 inches wide by 6 inches tall

Skills
Magic ring (14), Single Crochet (15), Increase (17), Decrease (17), Changing Colors, Chain (15), Crochet 2 Together (17), Back Loop Only (18), Slip Stitch (19)

Legs

Round 1: Mr8sc (8)
Round 2: 8inc (16)
Round 3-4: 16sc (16)
Round 5: 5sc, 3dec, 5sc (13)
Round 6: 4sc, dec, sc, dec, 4sc (11)

⎯ NOTE ⎯⎯⎯⎯⎯⎯⎯
Stuff until full
⎯⎯⎯⎯⎯⎯⎯⎯⎯⎯

Cut the yarn, make 2 pieces.

Arms

Round 1: Mr5sc (5)
Round 2: 5inc (10)
Round 3-5: 10sc (10)

Change to orange yarn

Round 6-10: 10sc (10)

Sew it up
Cut the yarn

 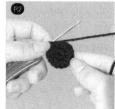 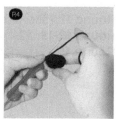 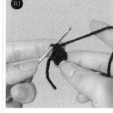  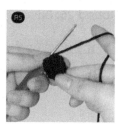
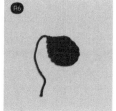    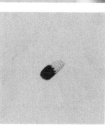

Head

Start with white yarn

Round 1: Mr8sc (8)
Round 2: 8inc (16)
Round 3: (sc, inc) repeat 8 times (24)
Round 4: BLO (2sc, inc) repeat 8 times (32)
Round 5: (3sc, inc) repeat 2 times, (sc, inc) repeat 7 times, (black) (sc, inc), (3sc, inc) repeat 2 times (44)
Round 6: (black) 10sc, (white) (2sc, inc) repeat 6 times, 2sc, (black) inc, 2sc, inc, 9sc, inc (53)
Round 7: (black) 12sc, (white) 23sc, (black) 18sc (53)
Round 8: (black) 14sc, (white) 20sc, (black) 19sc (53)
Round 9: (black) 15sc, (white) 18sc, (black) 20sc (53)
Round 10: (black) 16sc, (white) 16c, (black) 21sc (53)
Round 11: (black) 17sc, (white) 14sc, (black) 22sc (53)
Round 12: (black) 13sc, dec, 3sc, (white) 5sc, dec, 5sc, (black) 3sc, dec, 18sc (50)
Round 13: (black) 12sc, dec, 4sc, (white) 3sc, dec, 4sc, (black) 3sc, dec, 17sc (47)
Round 14: (black) 11sc, dec, 5sc, (white) 6sc, (black) 5sc, dec, 16sc (45)
Round 15: (black) 18s, (white) 4sc, (black) 23sc (45)
Round 16: (black) 19sc, (white) 2sc, (black) 24sc (45)
Round 17: (black) 19c, (white) dec, (black) 24sc (44)
Round 18-20: 44sc (44)
Round 21: (9sc, dec) repeat 4 times (40)
Round 22: 40sc (40)
Round 23: (3sc, dec) repeat 8 times (32)
Round 24: (2sc, dec) repeat 8 times (24)

- NOTE

Stuff until full

Round 25: (sc, dec) repeat 8 times (16)
Round 26: 8dec (8)

Cut the yarn and weave in the end.

Body

Start with orange yarn
Insert the hook into the BLO round of the head (Round 4)

Round 1: 24sc along the BLO round (24)
Round 2: (2sc, inc) repeat 8 times (32)
Round 3-4: 32sc (32)
Round 5: (3sc, inc) repeat 8 times (40)
Round 6-7: 40sc (40) change to black yarn
Round 8: BLO 40sc (40)
Round 9-10: 40sc (40)
Round 11: (3sc, dec) repeat 8 times (32)
Round 12-13: 32sc (32)
Round 14: (2sc, dec) repeat 8 times (24)

- NOTE

Stuff until full

Round 15: (sc, dec) repeat 8 times (16)
Round 16: 8dec (8)

Cut the yarn and weave in the end

 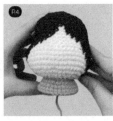 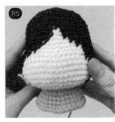

 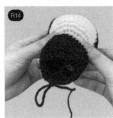

Hat

Round 1: Mr5sc (5)
Round 2-7: 5sc (5)
Round 8: 5inc (10)

Change to black yarn

Round 9: 10sc (10)

Change to orange yarn

Round 10: 10sc (10)
Round 11: (3sc, inc) repeat 2 times, 2sc (12)
Round 12: 12sc (12)

Change to black yarn

Round 13: 12sc (12)

Change to orange yarn

Round 14: (4sc, inc) repeat 2 times, 2sc (14)
Round 15: 14sc (14)
Round 16: (5sc, inc) repeat 2 times, 2sc (16)
Round 17: FLO 16sc (16)

Cut the yarn, leave a long tail for sewing

Ears

Round 1: Mr4sc (4)
Round 2: 4inc (8)
Round 3: (3sc, inc) repeat 2 times (10)
Round 4: (sc, inc) repeat 2 times (12)
Round 5: (5sc, inc) repeat 2 times (14)

Sew it up
Cut the yarn, leave long tail for sewing

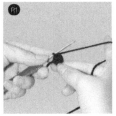  

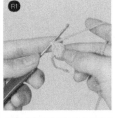 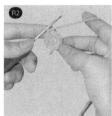 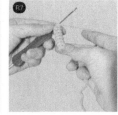

 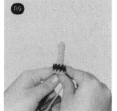 

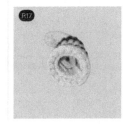 

Skirt

Insert the hook to the BLO round on the body (round 8)
2ch, (dc, dc-inc) repeat 18 times, 2hdc, 2sc, slst
*dc-inc: 2 together

Finish

- Attach the safety eyes, hat and ears to the head.
- Attach the arms and legs to the body.
- Sew the mouth by Black thread.

SCAN ME

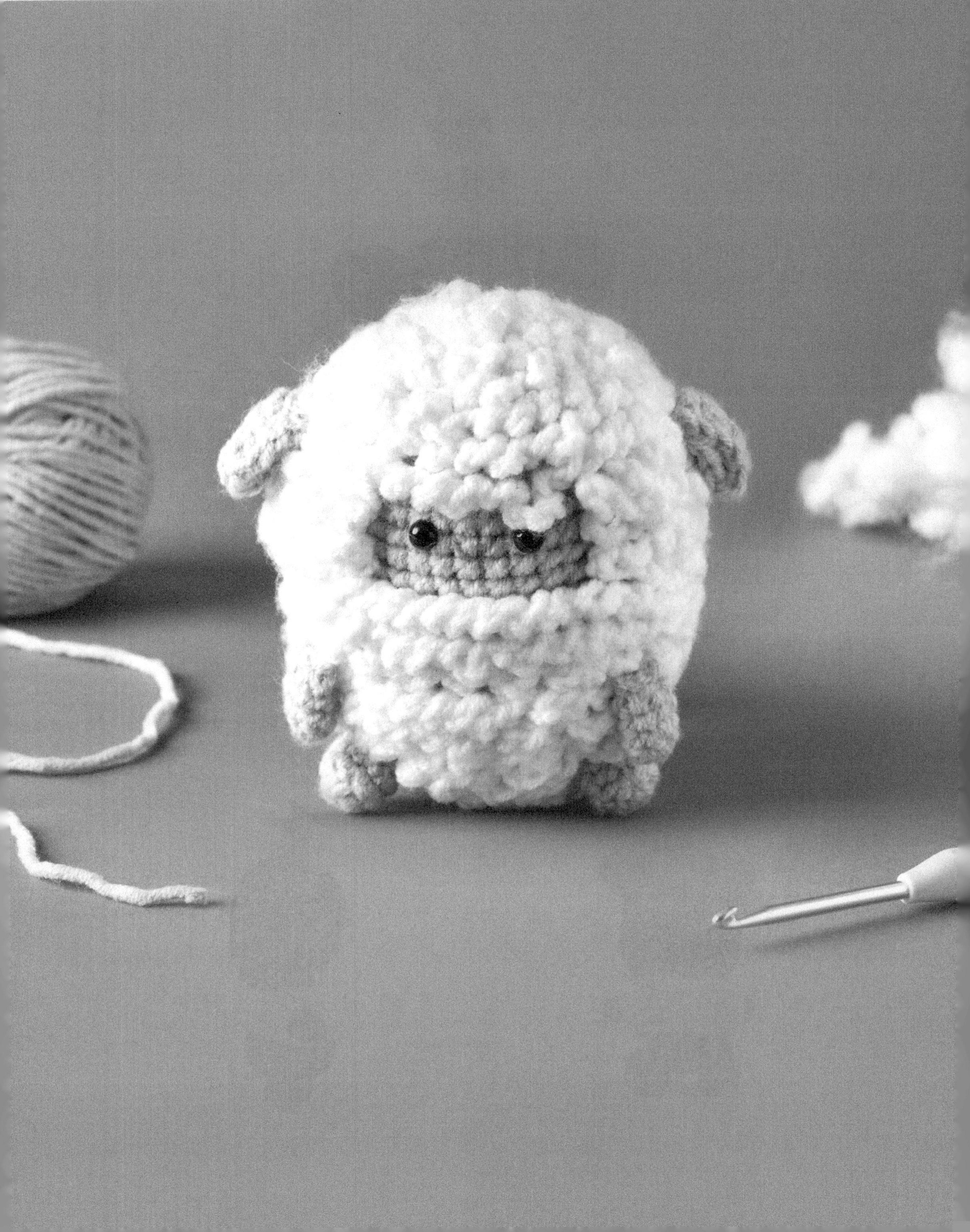

Happy The Sheep

(Difficult level 🧶 🧶 🧶 🧶)

Happy was Nana's most beloved pet. Happy's super thick fleece provided Nana with many cozy items for winter. One day, Nana played with Happy's wool, causing it to scatter all over the house, and her mother was very angry.

Materials

- Yarns (milk cotton): grey, white
- Stuffing
- Thread: Browm
- Safety eyes: 6mm
- Crochet hook 4.

Size

Approximately 3.5 inches wide by 6.5 inches tall

Skills

Magic ring (14), Single Crochet (15), Increase (17), Decrease (17), Back Loop Only (18), Double Crochet (21), Half Double Crochet (20)

Body

Round 1: Mr6sc
Round 2: Blo6inc
Round 3: Blo (sc, inc) repeat 6 times
Round 4: Blo (2sc, inc) repeat 6 times
Round 5: Blo (3sc, inc) repeat 6 times
Round 6: Blo (4sc, inc) repeat 6 times
Round 7: 36sc
Round 8: [blo (5sc, inc) repeat 2 times, 2sc] 8sc [blo 2sc, (inc, 5sc) repeat 2 times]
Round 9-11: [blo 15sc] 10sc [blo 15sc]
Round 12: [blo (6sc, inc) repeat 2 times, sc] 10sc [blo (inc, 6sc) repeat 2 times]
Round 13-17: Blo44sc
Round 18: Blo (9sc, dec) repeat 4 times
Round 19: Blo (8sc, dec) repeat 4 times
Round 20: Blo (4sc, dec) repeat 4 times
Round 21: Blo (3sc, dec) repeat 4 times
Round 22: Blo (2sc, dec) repeat 4 times

NOTE

Stuff until full

Round 23: Blo (sc, dec) repeat 4 times
Round 24: Blo6dec

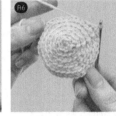
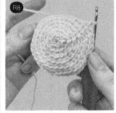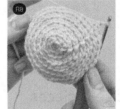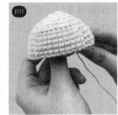

Sheep's wool

Start from the first front loop on the toe, up to 4 even stitches, crochet one single stitch into the next toe, repeat until finished

Arms

Round 1: Mr6sc
Round 2-4: 6sc

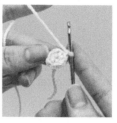 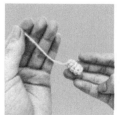 

Legs

Round 1: Mr8sc
Round 2: 8sc

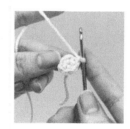  

Ears

Round 1: Mr5sc
Round 2: 5inc
Round 3: 2sc, 2hdc, 2dc, 2hdc, 2dc

--- NOTE ---

Make 2 pieces

  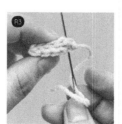

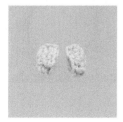

Finish

- Attach the safety eyes to the head of the sheep.
- Attach the arms and legs to the body.
- Sew the mouth by Brown thread.

SCAN ME

Flurry The Penguin

(Difficult level 🧶 🧶 🧶 🧶)

Flurry was known far for his bright orange wool sweater. One chilly day, he challenged his friends to a sliding race down the icy slopes. Little did he know, his sweater was so cozy that he slipped right past everyone, winning the race without even trying! His friends couldn't stop laughing at the sight of Flurry zooming by like a bright orange comet.

Materials

- Yarns (milk cotton): black, white, orange
- Stuffing
- Safety eyes: 6mm
- Crochet hook 4.

Size
Approximately 4 inches wide by 6.7 inches tall

Skills
Magic ring (14), Single Crochet (15), Increase (17), Decrease (17), Double Crochet 3 Together (21), Slip Stitch (20), Front Loop Only (18), Changing Colors.

Body

Round 1: Black, Mr8sc
Round 2: 8inc
Round 3: (sc, inc) repeat 8 times
Round 4: (3sc, inc) repeat 6 times
Round 5: (2sc, inc, 2sc) repeat 6 times
Round 6: (5sc, inc) repeat 6 times
Round 7: (3sc, inc, 3sc) repeat 6 times
Round 8-9: 48sc
Round 10: (3sc, dec, 3sc) repeat 6 times
Round 11-12: 42sc
Round 13-14: (orange 2sc, white sc) repeat 14 times

Change to orange yarn

Round 15: (5sc, dec) repeat 6 times
Round 16: 36sc

Change to white yarn

Round 17: 36sc

Change to orange yarn

Round 18: (4sc, dec) repeat 6 times
Round 19-20: 36sc

- NOTE -

Stuff until full

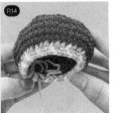  

Head

Round 1: Black, Mr8sc
Round 2: 8inc
Round 3: (sc, inc) repeat 8 times
Round 4: (sc, inc, sc) repeat 8 times
Round 5: (3sc, inc) repeat 8 times
Round 6: (2sc, inc, 2sc) repeat 8 times
Round 7: (5sc, inc) repeat 8 times
Round 8: (3sc, inc, 3sc) repeat 8 times
Round 9: 64sc
Round 10: Black 7sc, white 5sc, black 6sc, white 5sc, black 41sc
Round 11-12: Black 6sc, white 7sc, black 4sc, white 7sc, black 40sc
Round 13: Black 5sc, white 9sc, black 2sc, white 9sc, black 39sc
Round 14-16: Black 4sc, white 10sc, black 2sc, white 10sc, black 38sc
Round 17: Black (sc,inc) repeat 2 times, white (sc, inc) repeat 2 times, 6sc, black 2sc, white 6sc, (inc, sc) repeat 2 times, black (inc, sc) repeat 2 times, 34sc
Round 18-23: Black 6sc, white 26sc, black 40sc
Round 24: Black 6sc, white sc, dec, (7sc, dec) repeat 2 times, 5sc, black 2sc, dec, (7sc, dec) repeat 4 times
Round 25: Black 3sc, dec, 2sc, white 4sc, dec, 6sc, dec, 6sc, black dec, (6sc, dec) repeat 4 times, 3sc
Round 26: Black 5sc, dec, white (5sc, dec) repeat 2 times, 2X, black 3sc, dec, (5sc, dec) repeat 4 times
Round 27: Black 2sc, dec, 3sc, white sc, dec, 4sc, dec, 3sc, black sc, dec, (4sc, dec) repeat 4 times, 2sc

> **NOTE**
> **Stuff until full**

Round 28: Black (2sc, dec) repeat 10 times

Wings

Round 1: Black, Mr6sc
Round 2: 6inc
Round 3-4: 12sc
Round 5: (sc, inc) repeat 6 times
Round 6-7: 18sc
Round 8: (4sc, dec) repeat 3 times
Round 9: (3sc, dec) repeat 3 times
Round 10: 12sc

<u>Fold it and crochet 5sc to close, then sew it to the body.</u>

> **NOTE**
> **Connect the body and head:**
> **Sew on the inside**

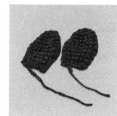

Mouth

Round 1: Orange, Mr10sc
Round 2: FLO10sc

Leave a long tail of yarn then sew it between rounds 17 & 20 on the head.

Legs

Round 1: Orange, Mr10sc
Round 2: FLO10sc

Leave a long tail of yarn then sew it between rounds 17 & 20 on the head.

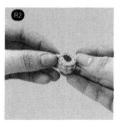 

Feet

Round 1: Orange, Mr5sc
Round 2: 5sc
Round 3: 5inc
Round 4: 10sc
Round 5: (sc, inc) repeat 5 times
Round 6: 15sc

Fold it in half and crochet 7sc
1ch, turn it over, (Sl, DC3TOG) repeat 3 times, Sl

Finish

- Sew the sole to the foot.
- Sew the nose to the head.
- Sew the 2 arms and 2 legs onto the body.
- Attach the safety eyes to the head.

SCAN ME

Tangtang The Bunny

(Difficult level 🧶🧶🧶🧶)

Tangtang, the chubby bunny, became renowned in the forest not only for his adorable appearance but also for his plump, round belly. Every morning, Tangtang would set up his mobile carrot shop, selling the freshest carrots to his forest friends.

Materials

- Yarns (milk cotton): beige, white, brown
- Stuffing
- Safety eyes: 6mm
- Crochet hook 4.

Size
Approximately 4 inches wide by 7 inches tall

Skills
Magic ring (14), Single Crochet (15), Increase (17), Decrease, (17) Front Loop Only (18), Slip Stitch (19), Back Loop Only (18), Changing Colors, Increase (2 Half Double Crochet) (20), Double Crochet (21), Single Crochet 3 Together (16)

Head

Round 1: Mr8sc
Round 2: 8inc
Round 3: (sc, inc) repeat 8 times
Round 4: (3sc, inc) repeat 6 times
Round 5: 30sc
Round 6: (2sc, inc, 2sc) repeat 6 times
Round 7-8: 36sc
Round 9: 11sc, 6inc, dec, 6inc, 11sc
Round 10-13: 47sc
Round 14: 10sc, 6dec, sc3tog, 6dec, 10sc
Round 15: (9sc, dec) repeat 3 times
Round 16: (3sc, dec) repeat 6 times
Round 17: (sc, dec, sc) repeat 6 times

- - NOTE - - - - - - - - - - - - - - - -

Stuff until full

- -

Round 18: (sc, dec) repeat 6 times

Ears

Round 1: 19ch, skip1, 5sc, 4hdc, 5f, 3hdc, w, 3hdc, 5dc, 4hdc, 5sc
Round 2: Insert wire and crochet 37sc
Sew the ears onto the head between rounds 3 and 4.

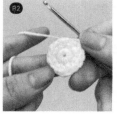   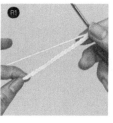  

Arms

Round 1: Mr7sc
Round 2-6: 7sc

Change to beige yarn to make the sleeves.

Round 7: BLO7inc
Round 8-11: 14sc

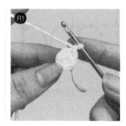
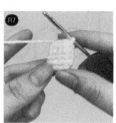

┌─ NOTE ─────────────────────┐

Stuff until full

└────────────────────────────┘

Round 12: 7dec
Round 13: Fold it in half, 3sc

At the FLO of round 7, crochet the ruffled edge
for the sweater: (3ch, sc) repeat 7 times

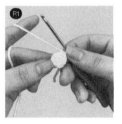
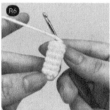
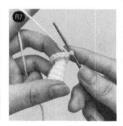

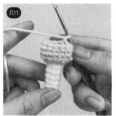

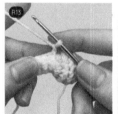

Hats

Round 1: Mr 8sc
Round 2: 8inc
Round 3: (sc, inc) repeat 8 times
Round 4: (2sc, inc) repeat 8 times
Round 5: (3sc, inc) repeat 8 times
Round 6: (4sc, inc) repeat 8 times
Round 7: (5sc, inc) repeat 8 times
Round 8: (6sc, inc) repeat 8 times
Round 9: (7sc, inc) repeat 8 times
Round 10-11: 72sc
Round 12: (7sc, dec) repeat 8 times
Round 13: 64sc
Round 14: (6sc, dec) repeat 8 times
Round 15: 54sc
Round 16: (5sc, dec) repeat 8 times
Round 17: 48sc
Round 18: 2sl, 2inc, 8TV, 2inc, 2sl
Round 19: 1ch, 2sl, 4sc, 16hdc, 4sc, 2sl

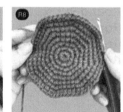

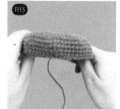

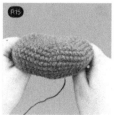
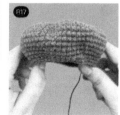

Legs

Round 1: Mr6sc
Round 2: 6inc
Round 3-6: 12sc
Round 7: 6dec

Sew the leg onto the body round 1.

Body

Start with brown yarn

Round 1: Mr6sc
Round 2: 6inc
Round 3: 12inc
Round 4: 24sc

Make 2 pieces

Round 5: Join the two parts together, 48sc
Round 6: (5sc, inc) repeat 8 times
Round 7-14: 56sc
Round 15: (5sc, dec) repeat 8 times
Round 16-17: 48sc
Round 18: (2sc, dec, 2sc) repeat 8 times
Round 19: 40sc
Round 20: FLO40sc, cut the yarn

Change to beige yarn

Blo40sc
Round 21: (3sc, dec) repeat 8 times
Round 22-23: 32sc
Round 24: (sc, dec, sc) repeat 8 times
Round 25-26: 24sc

> NOTE
>
> **Stuff until full**

Round 27: 12dec

Strap

Crochet into the BLO of the body, chain 16, then crochet into the BLO of the back of the body.

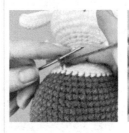

Finish

- Sew the two arms onto the body.
- Sew the mouth by Black thread.
- Attach the safety eyes to the head of the bunny.
- Attach a shirt button to the body where the strap meets.

SCAN ME

About the author

Ella Threadwell

f Ella Threadwell Crochet   ◎ Ella Threadwell Crochet
▶ Ella Threadwell Crochet   ♪ Ella Threadwell Crochet
✉ ellathreadwell@gmail.com

I am Ella Threadwell, a passionate crochet artist with over a decade of experience in the craft. From a young age, I found joy in creating intricate patterns and unique designs with just a hook and yarn. My work has been featured in numerous craft magazines and online platforms, inspiring thousands of crochet enthusiasts around the world. My love for crochet is matched only by my desire to share my knowledge and creativity with others.

In **"Animal Pals Crochet Book for Beginners: 20 Fun and Easy Step-by-Step Patterns for Making Adorable Animals,"** I bring my expertise to help beginners discover the charm of creating lovable animal friends. When I'm not crocheting, I enjoy spending time in nature, finding new inspiration for my next project. This book is a culmination of my years of dedication, designed to help both beginners and seasoned crafters alike discover the endless possibilities of crochet.

If you enjoyed this book, I would be incredibly grateful if you could leave a 5-star review on Amazon. Since this is my first book, I know it might have some small errors. If you have any feedback or see anything that didn't meet your expectations, please email me directly. Your detailed reviews will help me improve the book for future editions.

As a token of my appreciation for your valuable feedback, I would love to send you a small gift. Your feedback is invaluable and your support means the world for me. Thank you so much for purchasing this book and taking time to read it till the end.